GLOBE[TROTTER]

The best of BRUSSELS

FIONA NICHOLS

GLOBETROTTER™

First edition published in 2004
by New Holland Publishers (UK) Ltd
London • Cape Town • Sydney • Auckland
10 9 8 7 6 5 4 3 2 1

website: www.newhollandpublishers.com

Garfield House, 86 Edgware Road
London W2 2EA
United Kingdom

80 McKenzie Street
Cape Town 8001
South Africa

14 Aquatic Drive
Frenchs Forest, NSW 2086
Australia

218 Lake Road
Northcote, Auckland
New Zealand

Distributed in the USA by
The Globe Pequot Press, Connecticut

ISBN 1 84330 536 4

Publishing Manager (UK): Simon Pooley
Publishing Manager (SA): Thea Grobbelaar
DTP Cartographic Manager: Genené Hart
Editor: Melany McCallum
Cartographer: Nicole Engeler
Designer: Lellyn Creamer
Cover design: Lellyn Creamer, Nicole Engeler
Picture Researchers: Colleen Abrahams, Shavonne Johannes
Consultant: Belinda Levez
Proofreader: Thea Grobbelaar
Reproduction by Hirt & Carter (Pty) Ltd, Cape Town
Printed and bound in Hong Kong by Sing Cheong Printing Co. Ltd.

Photographic Credits:
Mark Azavedo: page 71;
Caroline Jones: pages 27, 63;
Image Link: title page, pages 6, 8, 12, 13, 15, 17, 18, 20, 22, 23, 24, 25, 26, 28, 29, 30, 31, 32, 34, 35, 36, 37, 38, 39, 40, 41, 45, 46, 48, 49, 52, 54, 65, 72, 77, 81, 84;
PhotoBank/Peter Baker: pages 53, 60;
Robin Smith: 11, 14, 50, 61, 80;
SC/Dorothy Burrows: page 33;
SC/Cees van Leeuwen: page 78;
SC/Chris North: page 21;
SC/Niall Riddell: cover, pages 7, 9, 16, 19, 47, 74;
SC/Jill Swanson: page 11;
SC/Geoffrey Taunton: pages 75, 79, 82, 83;
TI/Tony Page: page 76;
TI/Luc Janssens: page 42;
[SC = Sylvia Cordaiy Photo Library; TI = Travel Ink Photo Library]

Front Cover: *The Hôtel de Ville is magnificent at night time.*
Title Page: *A view over the canal basin at Dijver, Bruges.*

CONTENTS

MAKE THE MOST OF YOUR GUIDE

Reading these two pages will help you to get the most out of your guide and save you time when using it. Sites discussed in the text are cross-referenced with the cover maps – for example, the reference 'Map C–D4' refers to the Central Brussels Map (Map C), column D, row 4. Use the Map Plan below to quickly locate the map you need.

MAP PLAN

Outside Back Cover | Outside Front Cover

Inside Front Cover | Inside Back Cover

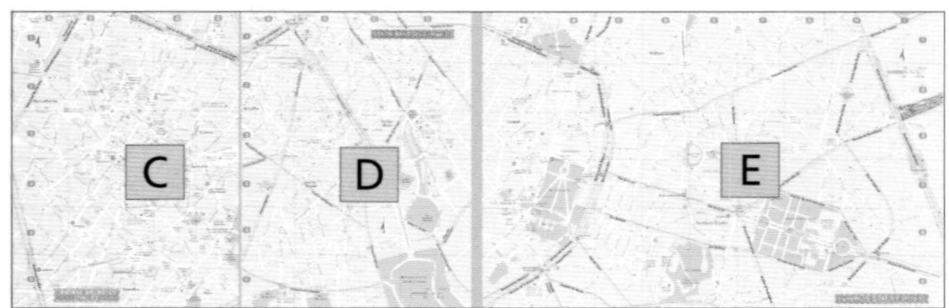

THE BIGGER PICTURE

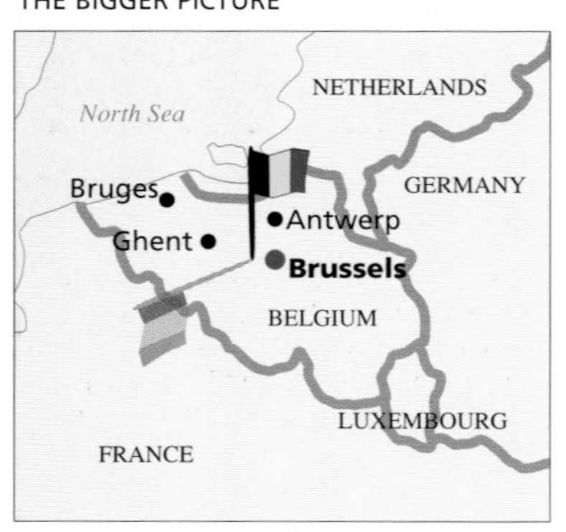

Key to Map Plan

A – Around Brussels
B – Brussels Métro and Prémétro
C – Central Brussels
D – South Brussels
E – European Quarter
F – Bruges
G – Ghent
H – Antwerp
I – Laeken and Heysel

Key to Symbols

✉ — address	⌚ — opening times
☎ — telephone	🚌 — tour
fax	💰 — entry fee
💻 — website	🍽 — restaurants nearby
e-mail address	M — métro or prémétro station

Map Legend

motorway		main road	Blvd d'Anvers
national road		pedestrian mall	RUE NEUVE
main road		other road	Rue du Midi
minor road		métro	Merode M
railway		prémétro	P
river	Zenne	one way street	
route number	A4	built-up area	
city	BRUSSELS	ferry boat	
major town	Tienen	building of interest	La Bourse
town	Waterloo	library	
large village	Holsbeek	post office	
village	Duisberg	parking area	P
area name	Ixelles	tourist information	i
airport		place of worship	Saint Nicolas
battlesite	Battle of Waterloo	police station	
place of interest	Manneken Pis	bus terminus	
hotel	H NOGA	hospital	
tunnel		park & garden	Jardins d'Egmont

Keep us Current

Travel information is apt to change, which is why we regularly update our guides. We'd be most grateful to receive feedback from you if you've noted something we should include in our updates. If you have any new information, please share it with us by writing to the Publishing Manager, Globetrotter, at the office nearest to you (addresses on the imprint page of this guide). The most significant contribution to each new edition will be rewarded with a free copy of the updated guide.

Above: *The Parc de Bruxelles is a fine public park, in front of the country's parliament.*

BRUSSELS

Capital of Belgium, Brussels is situated at the heart of this largely low-lying country. Although an urban settlement took form over a millennium ago, the city has risen to the fore in the last couple of decades as the European Union has swollen its ranks and many of its institutions and international companies have made their home in this pleasant yet still small city. Brussels, like Belgium, is largely unknown beyond its national borders but this capital city, easy to negotiate by foot or by public transport, packs a punch which matches if not surpasses many of its European peers. Music, cuisine, beer mania, museums, parks and some beautiful architecture ensure any visit to the Belgian capital is a memorable one.

Climate

Belgium has a northern climate: the weather is rarely predictable. There are four seasons, though they tend to merge from one to the other. **Winter** is inevitably cold and sometimes rainy, and though snow is rare, it can fall occasionally in Brussels. **Spring** is a fine time to visit: cool, with the odd shower, yet it can also be sunny and warm. **Summer** temperatures can rise above 30°C (86°F) though they usually hover around 24°C (75°F). The occasional thunder shower might freshen the streets. **Autumn** is a pleasant time: the parks are beautifully painted with golden leaves and the days are still warmish despite shortening in length.

The Land

Parks provide welcome areas of greenery in the centre of Brussels and give the city a shot of much needed fresh air. The parks are largely deciduous (chestnut, beech, oak or sycamore) and therefore tend to be somewhat bare in winter. As they are rather short on flowers, they are at their best in spring, summer or autumn. **Wildlife** is minimal in the city parks, but around the forested areas of Soignes or Cambre there is some semi-rural bird life.

History in Brief

Belgium's past reflects much of the history of Europe, with its long struggles between empires, feudal towns, the aristocracy, dukes, princedoms and colonizing powers.

Julius Caesar extended Rome's reach to include the area inhabited by the Celtic tribe, the Belgae. But the territory fell to the **Merovingians** under Clovis I and they ruled the area until **Charlemagne** founded the Carolingian dynasty in 768. On his death the Western Empire was divided among his three sons and the geographical area we know today as Belgium fell between two heirs. In the ensuing years the **Counts of Flanders** rose to prominence and, under their strong influence, fortified towns were built to protect locals from invading northerners. Ghent, Bruges and Ypres took form. The southeast of the country fell under the **Duchy of Lorraine** and in 977 Charles, Duke of Lorraine, built a fortress that was to become the foundations of Brussels.

The **Norse** invasions were rebuffed and gradually stability settled on the land. **Trade**, in particular the importation of wool from England and the subsequent exportation of fabric, grew rapidly and the cities of Flanders prospered. It was the rise of the great guilds and a period of rich cultural diversity. However, the aristocracy were little pleased and took the cities to task, but were defeated at the historic **Battle of the Golden Spurs** in 1302. The tables were turned again a few years later when the French Counts regained control of Flanders.

Facts about Belgium
Population: Brussels, 955,000 inhabitants; Antwerp, 450,000; Ghent, 225,000; Charleroi, 202,000; Liège, 187,000; Bruges, 116,000; Namur, 105,000.
Rivers: Leie (Lys in French); Meuse; Schelde (Escaut in French and Scheldt in English).
Provinces: 10.
Government: A federal system implemented in 1992.

Below: *Despite its central location, the Royal Palace is not occupied by the royal family: it is used for state functions.*

Waterloo
From the top of the 45m (145ft) hill known as **Butte du Lion**, the Lion of Waterloo, you get an expansive view of battlefields comprising the three main farmhouses in the midst of the battle, and the villages of Braine l'Alleud, Genappe, Plancenoit and Waterloo.

Napoleon spent the night of Saturday, 17 June 1815 at Vieux Grappe while Wellington slept in Waterloo (his 125,000-man army was stationed around the farm of Mont St Jean). Troops took up their positions the following morning. Battle began at 11:30 as the French attacked but they were repeatedly pushed back by the British and the Prussians. By 20:30 the French were in flight, Napoleon barely escaping with his life. And at 21:00 Wellington and Blücher congratulated each other on their success. In terms of human cost, 13,000 lost their lives and 35,000 were injured.

Towards the end of the **Hundred Years' War**, the Burgundian empire expanded and flourished under **Philip the Good**. On Philip's death in 1467 the region passed into the omnipotent hands of **Charles V** and then, in 1555, to **Philip II**. An ardent Catholic, Philip's rule clashed with the rise of Europe's nascent Protestantism and resulted in rebellion, repression and executions. Among the thousands of fatal casualties were the counts de Hornes and d'Egmont. For decades the two religious groups warred and by the end of the 16th century **William of Orange** held the United Provinces in the north of the country, and Spain held sway over the Catholic regions in the south – the Spanish Netherlands.

Under **Louis XIV** the French made various attempts to take the Spanish Netherlands, which displeased the Dutch and the English. The **War of the Spanish Succession** (1702–1713) left the Belgian territory again open to claim and Louis was the strongest contender, but at the end of his reign his hand was forced by the Dutch, English and Austrians and, under the **Treaty of Utrecht**, France ceded its claims in favour of the Austrian **Habsburgs**. The arrangement suited the Belgians but within a few decades, as the French Revolution fomented, the Belgians also sought independence. Austria naturally opposed the movement but in 1795 the region fell to the French, and the cities' wealth was pillaged and ruined.

Twenty years later **Napoleon** lost Belgium in his historic defeat at **Waterloo**. Under **William of Orange**, the Dutch claimed the territory but were finally run

out of town when Brussels rose in revolt, and in January 1831 Belgium was declared an independent nation.

Leopold of Saxe-Coburg was chosen as the first monarch and under this king, and then his son, **Leopold II**, the country flourished. It acquired its only colony, the **Congo**. **Albert I** ruled through World War I and was succeeded by his son **Leopold III** who tried, despite the odds, to lead the country under German occupation during World War II, but reluctantly had to relinquish control by surrendering to the enemy. In 1950 Leopold abdicated and his son, **Baudouin**, succeeded him. **Albert II** assumed the throne on the death of his brother a few years ago. The country has continued to grow in prosperity, stature and importance, much enhanced in its position as 'capital of Europe'.

Above: *Glassy and modern, the European Parliament.*
Opposite: *Belgium's much loved King Baudouin.*

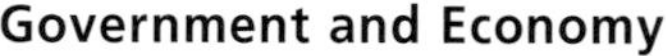

Government and Economy

Belgium has a complex system of government as it is split into three federal districts: **Flanders, Wallonia** and **Brussels Capital**. The city of Brussels is predominantly French-speaking despite being located, geographically, in the heart of Wallonia, a Dutch-speaking region. Brussels is furthermore divided into 19 **communes** with various levels of autonomy. Brussels is also the seat of the national government responsible for such national matters as state security, finance and foreign relations. Although the country has a much loved **monarchy** (the younger members of the Royal family are popular though not particularly 'regal'

Diamonds

Crystallized carbon, near flawless, is the start of a glittering diamond. In their raw form they look like glass pebbles, but with skilled cutting – into the now-famous 58-facet Antwerp cut that constitutes the classic shape – and polishing, these rocks become gems.

Diamonds were first cut in **Antwerp** in 1476. With their dominance of the trade route to India, Portuguese Jews developed the industry. Zaïrese, Lebanese and Indians assumed important positions when South African stones were discovered.

Diamonds are categorized by the four Cs: **clarity** (lack of flaws), **cut** (quality of facets), **carat** (weight) and **colour** (from gin-clear to blues and pinks).

Above: *People-watching from one of the Grand-Place's many cafés.*

figures), the day-to-day business of running the country is handled by the two-house **parliament**: the 182-member **Senate** and the 212-strong **Chamber of Representatives**. The **prime minister** is chosen from the political party holding the majority of power in the lower house of parliament.

Belgians are justifiably proud of their lifestyle and Brussels is its showcase. Though many of its residents are foreigners (some 250,000 live in the city), its restaurants, cafés, shops and nightlife mirror a healthy, expanding economy. The principal **exports** are in machinery and transport equipment, chemicals, metals and food products. The diamond trade is also one of the country's major sources of revenue.

Famous Belgians

Jacques Brel, singer and songwriter
Liz Claibourne, fashion designer
César Franck, composer
Arthur Grumiaux, classical pianist
Audrey Hepburn, actress and ambassadress
Hergé, author of Tintin
Maurice Maeterlink, playwright and author
Hercule Poirot, Christie's fictional detective
Django Reinhardt, gypsy guitarist
Georges Simenon, author of the detective stories featuring Maigret

The People

A first-time visit to the country and contact with its people (many speak English) is usually a real eye-opener. The Bruxellois are courteous, often well educated, cultured and sometimes misunderstood. They work hard, and relax with equal enthusiasm, giving the city its evening and weekend buzz.

The Language

Linguistically speaking, Belgium is one of Europe's more complex countries (*see* page 91). Historically created from a number of distinctly different dukedoms, kingdoms, empires and colonies, its people speak **Dutch** (previously called Flemish), **French**

and, in the southeast of the country, **German**. With a continuing friction between the various linguistic communities that govern different cultural attitudes, there is still reluctance to speak the language of a neighbouring community. Although it is officially bilingual, in practice Brussels is largely French-speaking. It is not uncommon to hear four or five languages spoken around a business table or in a restaurant, and most people can speak English, some almost fluently: a reassuring situation for the Anglophone visitor.

Brussels, Brussel or Bruxelles?
Belgium has two official languages – Dutch and French – although we have opted for the anglicized form of the better-known places. Thus we speak of Brussels (Brussel in Dutch or Bruxelles in French), Ghent (Gent or Gand in French), Antwerp (Antwerpen in Dutch and Anvers in French), Bruges (Brugge), Ypres (Ieper), Flanders (Vlaanderen) and Ostend (Oostende).

Religion

The two main faiths of the Belgians are **Catholicism** and **Protestantism**. There are **churches** to both communities in Brussels, although those built in the name of Catholicism outnumber the rest. With its wide immigrant population, there are also **mosques**, **temples** and **synagogues** catering to the spiritual requirements of its varied residents.

The Arts

Belgium is home to three important eras in European art: **Gothic** architecture, **Early Flemish** painting and sculpture, and the **Art Nouveau** movement. In between the latter two, three artists of the highest order coloured the homes and churches of Belgium and beyond with their magnificent works.

In the late 14th and early 15th centuries much of Belgian architecture took form, creating the footprints for today's handsome towns.

Below: *A detail from the ornate gable of the Old Recorder's House.*

Peter Paul Rubens
Rubens entered Antwerp's Guild of painters in 1598 but left for Italy in 1600. He was influenced by the prolific artworks in Rome, notably those of Caravaggio. In 1608, he returned to Antwerp where, up to then, painting in Flanders had only been on a small scale. He brought with him a feeling for large-scale decoration, the Italian confidence which brought out a strength of character in his classical and allegorical subjects. Rubens was employed by the Spanish as Court Painter to the Spanish Governors in the Netherlands and through his diplomatic yet humble attitude, did much to mend Anglo-Hispanic relations. Twenty years his junior, **Anthony van Dyck** was his most notable assistant and pupil. He also taught **Jordaens** and **Snyders**.

Ghent, **Antwerp** and particularly **Bruges** have some magnificent examples of Gothic architecture, redolent with sculpture and moulded details all dating from this period. Brussels' **Grand-Place** is a virtual museum-piece (albeit much renovated), while other city buildings such as the **Nôtre-Dame du Sablon** and the **Cathedral** (*see* pages 22 and 27) were also started at this time.

For many it is the artists that we now call the **Flemish Primitives** who attract the most attention. **Jan van Eyck** (1390–1441) rose to immense acclaim within the Burgundian court, leaving us with many works among which is his stunning altarpiece in the **Cathedral of St Bavon** (*see* page 82). Contemporary with Van Eyck was **Robert Campin** (1375–1444) – possibly the elusive painter known as the **Master of Flémalle** – and **Rogier van der Weyden** (1399–1464). Look out also for the slightly stylized work of **Dirk Bouts** (1415–1475) who was much influenced by Van der Weyden. More fine works were produced by **Petrus Christus** (d 1472/3), **Hugo van der Goes** (d 1482/3) and **Hans Memling** (1430/40–1494) in Bruges, and the last master of the Bruges style, **Gerard David** (d 1523).

A few years later the **Brueghel** (also spelled Bruegel) family came to the fore. The very talented **Pieter Brueghel the Elder** (1525–1569) created a name for himself with his peasant scenes and satirical subjects and was followed by his son, **Pieter Brueghel the Younger** (1564–1638), and his brother, **Jan** (1568–1625), a master miniaturist and renowned court painter.

Peter Paul Rubens (1577–1640) was to change the face of painting yet again in

the 17th century. Diplomat and painter, he created some huge and emotive masterpieces (*see* pages 24 and 79) and influenced one of his assistants, **Anthony van Dyck** (1599–1641), who subsequently forged his own style. The third great painter of this trilogy was **Jacob Jordaens** (1593–1678), another assistant to Peter Paul Rubens.

Above: *A plaque to the memory of Charles Buls, the mayor of Brussels during the Art-Nouveau years.*
Opposite: *A self-portrait by Rubens.*

It was **Art Nouveau** that changed the profile of Brussels at the beginning of the 20th century. Under the leadership of **Victor Horta** (1861–1947), talented young artists such as **Henry van de Velde** and **Paul Hanka** took up the movement started by English craftsmen, using plants as their theme. Glass, steel, wood and fabrics took on a quasi-organic form and Brussels' wealthy elite was seduced by elaborate interiors and fresh architectural perspectives, commissioning homes and commercial buildings. Sadly, the movement lasted little more than a decade but many of its buildings – and art forms – still survive.

Belgium has continued to produce notable artists. **René Magritte** (1898–1967) fronted the Belgian **Surrealist** movement, while painter **Paul Delvaux** (1897–1994) had success with his rather vacant, statuesque figures. **James Ensor** (1860–1949) followed in the **Impressionist** footsteps and later developed his own brand of **Expressionism**. Look out also for works by **Rik Wouters** (1882–1916), **Victor Serveranckx** (1887–1945) and **Ferdinand Schirren** (1872–1944). The **Musée d'Art Moderne** (*see* page 25) has a good selection of their work.

Almshouses

Almshouses are one of Belgium's more interesting examples of domestic architecture. They were built in those prosperous days of the 14th and 15th centuries by guilds for their ageing members and members' widows, or by wealthy citizens for the less fortunate. They were usually conceived as a series of low buildings around a central courtyard with a communal garden and a chapel. Some are still running as homes for the elderly.

See Map C–C4 ★★★

Above: *Site of the annual flower show, Grand-Place is transformed every August.*
Opposite: *Hôtel de Ville, with its 96m (315ft) spire, dominates Grand-Place.*

GRAND-PLACE

This is Baroque grandeur on a large scale. Built in 1695 after the French managed, in three short days, to raze every building except the Town Hall, the houses that rim this square are simply magnificent. They were constructed as *maisons des corporations* – guildhouses – and many still carry signs of their former trades.

The large open space (not a sculpture or fountain breaks the cobblestone ground) is perennially filled with visitors who come to marvel at this unique architectural heritage. Perhaps the best way to appreciate the square is to lunch at one of the restaurant terraces or to stop for a drink at a café on the northern side. From the comfort of a chair, you are well placed to take in the gilded statues of saints and heroes of yore, appreciate the glistening architectural details and marvel at the intricacy (and exaggeration) of some of the designs.

In even-numbered years Brussels has its August (second weekend) **flower show** and the cobblestones are covered with a breathtaking carpet of potted azaleas. At other times, early risers can visit the flower market which is lively in the mornings. By night, too, this large square lives – not only because of its restaurants, bars and taverns, but with the nightly *son et lumière* performances where music and lights surround the Town Hall. It's worth coming back for dinner or a stroll.

Grand-Place
✉ Grand-Place, B-1000, Brussels
🖳 www.tib.be
🕒 Daily; flower market in mornings.
🚌 *See* page 49 for bus tours.
🍽 Plenty of cafés, bars and restaurants in and around the square.
M Bourse or Gare Centrale

See Map C–C4	★★★

HÔTEL DE VILLE

Competently cleaned to its former creamy colour, this stunningly decorated **Town Hall** must rate among the most impressive buildings in Europe. It is the only building in the **Grand-Place** to date back to the Middle Ages.

What is now the **east wing** was begun in the first decade of the 15th century to house guild representatives and a burgermeister (mayor). In 1444 the building was extended with a **west wing**. When this was completed in 1449, Jan van Ruysbroeck added the amazing tower. Spend some time admiring the array of sculpture representing Medieval and Renaissance nobility. This was finally completed in the 19th century.

The interior courtyard, again finished off in Baroque style, affords an upward contemplation to the Town Hall's tower, elegantly rising up towards the gilded weather vane. Behind the building, in Rue de l'Amigo, stood the **Amigo Prison** (now a luxury hotel) and there is still a tunnel connecting the former prison and the Town Hall.

Hôtel de Ville
✉ Grand-Place,
B-1000, Brussels
☎ 02 279 43 65
Fax 02 513 83 20
www.tib.be
Visits by guided tour only. English-language tours 15:15, 15:45 Tue, Wed, 10:45, 12:15 Sun (except in winter); tours in French 14:30 Tue, Wed, 11:30 Sun.
See page 49
Entrance fee, discount for groups of over 12 persons.
Restaurants in the square and in neighbouring areas.
M Bourse or Gare Centrale

La Maison du Roi
⊠ Grand-Place, B-1000, Brussels
☎ 02 279 43 50
02 279 43 62
10:00–17:00 Tue–Sat, 10:00–13:00 Wed
See page 49 for guided tours.
Entrance fee; reduction for groups over 12 people.
Scores of restaurants, cafés and bars in and around the Grand-Place.
M Bourse or Gare Centrale

See Map C–D4 | ★★★

LA MAISON DU ROI

The huge building directly opposite the Town Hall is La Maison du Roi which houses the **Musée de la Ville de Bruxelles**. Its origins date back to the 13th century when it was a baker's guildhouse (*Halle au Pain*). It served as offices for Brabant's Receiver General, a duke, and its name was changed to the Maison du Duc. Later, however, he became King of Spain so the building changed its name yet again. All very misleading as the king never actually lived here. What we see today is a late 19th-century construction built in neo-Gothic style. Inside, an eclectic collection documents the city of Brussels through paintings, including a fine Rubens sketch for a tapistry, some early Flemish painting and the huge collection of clothes for the Manneken Pis (*see* page 19).

Other guildhouses (*see* page 44) of note around this square include the **Maison des Boulangers**, a small classically styled house at no. 1, and the house known as **Le Sac**, at no. 4, which was built in 1644 for the joiners and coopers. The tools of their trade can be seen under the windows. At no. 7, the **Maison du Renard**, the haberdashers erected their guildhouse with a statue of Saint Nicolas on the top. The **Maison du Cygne** at no. 9 dates from 1698 and was the butchers' guildhouse, while the **Golden Boat** at no. 25 belonged to the tailors' guild.

Below: *Rebuilt in neo-Gothic style in 1872, the Maison du Roi is another landmark building on the Grand-Place.*

See Map C–D3/4 ★★★

QUARTIER DE L'ILOT SACRÉ

Radiating from the Grand-Place, the ancient streets of this neighbourhood recall their original trades: for the butter sales, **Rue au Beurre**; meats and bread in the **Rue Chair et Pain**, chickens in the **Rue du Marché aux Poulets**; the coal market, **Rue du Marché au Charbon**; herrings in the **Rue des Harengs**; and the open-air square where herbs and plants were once sold, the **Marché aux Herbes**.

Above: *Fish and seafood are ever popular, especially in Brussels.*

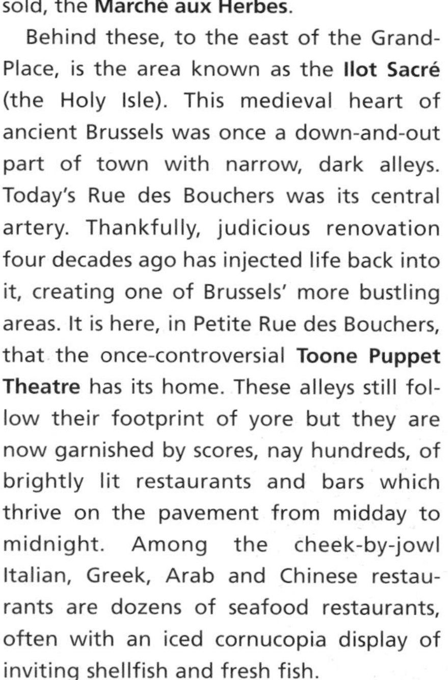

Behind these, to the east of the Grand-Place, is the area known as the **Ilot Sacré** (the Holy Isle). This medieval heart of ancient Brussels was once a down-and-out part of town with narrow, dark alleys. Today's Rue des Bouchers was its central artery. Thankfully, judicious renovation four decades ago has injected life back into it, creating one of Brussels' more bustling areas. It is here, in Petite Rue des Bouchers, that the once-controversial **Toone Puppet Theatre** has its home. These alleys still follow their footprint of yore but they are now garnished by scores, nay hundreds, of brightly lit restaurants and bars which thrive on the pavement from midday to midnight. Among the cheek-by-jowl Italian, Greek, Arab and Chinese restaurants are dozens of seafood restaurants, often with an iced cornucopia display of inviting shellfish and fresh fish.

Quartier de l'Ilot Sacré
✉ Rue des Bouchers up to the Marchés des Herbes
🕒 daily
🚌 *See* page 49
🍽 Scores of restaurants open from midday to midnight and later. Peruse a number of menus before making a final choice.
M Bourse, De Brouckère or Gare Centrale

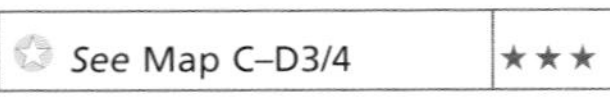

See Map C–D3/4 ★★★

Below: *The airy and spectacular Galerie du Roi.*

GALERIES SAINT HUBERT

One of the most impressive architectural features of Brussels, the 210m (230yd) long Saint Hubert Galleries is a series of gloriously light, glass-covered, neoclassical shopping arcades inspired by Paris' Palais Royale and evoking Milan's chic Galleria Vittorio Emanuele II. The complex is just one of the 18 galleries to be found in the city. They were built in 1847 on the plans drawn up by J P Clysenaer and because of their confection of iron and glass – an indoor-outdoor ambience – were a first in Europe.

The galleries are divided into three; the **Galerie du Roi** (the King's Gallery) which meets Rue des Bouchers and then becomes **Galerie de la Reine** (Queen's Gallery), and the smaller **Galerie des Princes** (Princes' Gallery) which branches off at a tangent. They run from the Rue d'Arenberg down to the popular **Place Agora** (where the contemporary Galerie de l'Agora has none of the former's charm). Comprising six different floors (from cellars to attics), they have been designed to appear to rise through three floors only, enforced by the decorative details in Ionic, Doric and Corinthian orders.

These galleries are one of the city's best addresses for smart boutiques, bookstores, *chocolatiers* and for lingering over a coffee or apéritif while people-watching.

Galeries Saint Hubert
✉ Les Galeries Saint Hubert, B-1000, Brussels
Free of charge.
Cafés located in the galleries, and plenty of restaurants in the neighbourhood.
M Gare Centrale

See Map C–C4 ★★★

MANNEKEN PIS

It is an unlikely highlight but whatever you might do to play it down, this small statue of a chubby child urinating into a fountain at the corner of two roads continues to attract camera-toting crowds in much the same fashion as does Rome's Trevi Fountain.

Sometimes called 'Brussels' oldest citizen', the Manneken Pis dates from 1619 when it was sculpted by **Jerôme Duquesnoy L'Ancien**, but in fact this small bronze statuette (and it is much smaller than you imagine – most people are disappointed in the tiny piddler) is a replacement for the original, which was stolen and smashed by a French ex-convict in 1747.

Interestingly, the statue has a series of costumes for ceremonial occasions. **King Louis XV** of France was the first to offer a suit and subsequently the little boy has acquired over 500 costumes – varying from Elvis's white trousers to Asian mandarin robes – in which he is dressed on appropriate days. These are on display in a room at the **Musée de la Ville de Bruxelles** (*see* page 16) while replicas of various costumes and myriad copies of the statue itself are on sale all around this neighbourhood.

The feminists who enquire whether or not there is an equivalent female version may be surprised to learn that **Jeanneke Pis**, his female counterpart, is at the **Petit Sablon**.

Manneken Pis
✉ Corner of Rue de l'Etuve and Rue du Chêne, B-1000, Brussels
www.tib.be
See page 49
Free of charge.
Plenty of cafés and restaurants in nearby Grand-Place.
M Gare Centrale

Below: *A change of clothes for the small Manneken Pis.*

Les Places Sablon
✉ Place du Grand Sablon, or Rue de la Régence, B-1000, Brussels
💻 www.tib.be
🚌 *See page 49*
🍽 Many smart cafés and restaurants in this large square.
M Gare Centrale

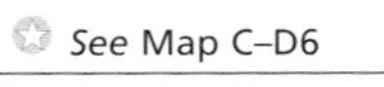

See Map C–D6 ★★★

LES PLACES SABLON
Place du Grand Sablon

'The Large Sand Place' is an odd name for one of the city's premiere squares. The name derives from its once sandy soil. The slightly sloping square rises uphill to the supremely elegant church, **Nôtre-Dame du Sablon** (*see* page 22), that dominates the top end of the square and looks out onto its smaller and garden-filled sister square, the **Place du Petit Sablon**. The elegant Place du Grand Sablon is known for its lively Saturday and Sunday antiques market (*see* page 21 for details) and for its myriad cafés, bars and restaurants. Well-heeled Belgians can be seen shopping in the patisseries, *traiteurs*, *chocolatiers* or antique shops – some of the best in town.

Place du Petit Sablon

This placid square is a favourite with local lunchers who relax in the beautifully kept gardens. Surrounding this tranquil spot is a fine wrought-iron fence with 48 bronze statuettes representing the city's guilds. In the upper part of the gardens, two sculptures honour Flemish patriots **counts** of **Hornes** and **Egmont** who were hung by the Spaniards in 1568 in the Grand-Place. To the southwest of the square is the Palais d'Egmont, formerly the count's residence but now used for government offices.

Below: *The small but pretty gardens of the Place du Petit Sablon attract a lunch-time crowd.*

See Map C	★★★

SUNDAY MARKETS

Not a site, but a major event on the weekend agenda, the Sunday antiques (read bric-a-brac) markets are among the city's highlights.

Pick of the chic is the market on **Place du Grand Sablon**. Competing with the smart shops in the area selling antiques, home furnishings and art, stalls on the square sell china, coins, decorative items and various other collectables.

Above: *The Sunday markets around Brussels are the haunt of local and international bargain hunters.*

For a wide range of goods at the bric-a-brac end of the spectrum, head for the **Place du Jeu de Balle**, in the Marolles district. Goods are unloaded on Thursday mornings (07:00) and the show goes on till Sunday. It pays to get there early. Between these two markets run the parallel **Rue Blaes** and **Rue Haute**. This is a collector's haven, rising in quality and price the nearer it gets to the Places Sablon. Numerous antique shops of all classes and qualities, Asian knick-knacks, modern furniture and household items tempt even the untemptable. These shops, too, are open throughout the week, though they close earlier on Sundays.

Beyond the city walls, the aficionados head for the flea market at the **Abattoirs d'Anderlecht** (rue Ropsy Chaudron 24). At **St Gilles** (Rue du Fort), too, there is a weekend flea market. On Sunday mornings, the covered market in **Rue Vanderkindere**, Uccle, is the place to be. Lastly, **Auderghem** has a Sunday market – held in a different place each week. Check out its locations with the tourist office.

Daily Markets
Look out for the following markets: **Place Ste Catherine**, daily for fruit and veg; **Grand-Place** daily for flowers and plants and its Sunday morning bird market; **Place Flagey** (Ixelles) for its daily morning produce market, and **Gare du Midi** for its general Sunday morning market.

See Map C–D6 ★★★

Above: *The beautiful stained-glass windows of the church of Nôtre-Dame du Sablon.*

NÔTRE-DAME DU SABLON

Carefully renovated, this 15th–16th-century Gothic building dominates the top end of the Place du Grand Sablon. Although much has been restored, in some cases entirely replaced, its graceful exterior and its magnificent stained-glass windows are a pleasure to look at. The church dates back to 1304 when the guild of **Arbalesters**, crossbowmen, built a chapel on this sandy hill to venerate a statue of Our Lady brought from Antwerp and believed to have miraculous powers. This was their neck of woods and, in the 17th century, these supershots sometimes held competitions in the square.

Among the many points of interest in Nôtre-Dame du Sablon are the **stained-glass windows** in the choir, rising some 15m (47ft). Some of them have been entirely renovated and almost all of them are magnificent. The stories that they relate are, to most visitors, of little importance, for the quality of workmanship and the patterns of colour speak volumes.

Note too the Baroque chapel by the choir. Elaborately decorated, this was erected to house the mortal remains of a prominent Brussels family – the **Tour et Tassis**, renowned for having founded Brussels' international postal service.

Nôtre-Dame du Sablon
✉ Rue Bodenbroeck 6, B-1000, Brussels
☎ 02 511 57 41
Fax 02 514 25 26
⏲ 09:00–18:00 Mon–Fri and Sun, 10:00–18:00 Sat
🚌 *See page 49*
💰 Entrance fee for entering the choir.
🍽 Plenty of restaurants in Place du Grand Sablon.
M Gare Centrale or Porte de Namur

See Map E–A5 ★★★

PLACE ROYALE

The graceful Royal Square is a focal point of regal Brussels and lies above the sloping **Mont des Arts**, the link between the Lower Town (the historic heart of Brussels) and the Upper Town (built later). In its centre stands a statue of **Godfrey de Bouillon**, one of the first crusaders.

Place Royale is located where the 15th-century **Coudenberg Palace** once stood – little remains of this once lavish home of the Dukes of Burgundy, which is open for visits twice weekly. Here, the classically inspired church of **St Jacques sur Coudenberg** ensures that the name, at least, is not lost. It is a pleasant and airy church with a certain noble simplicity. It also served as a court of law for a short period of time before reverting to its ecclesiastical function.

Beyond the church, and just off the Place Royale, is the **Musée de la Dynastie**, housed in the **Hôtel de Bellevue**, an elegant palatial building that has seen service as a princely residence and a luxury hotel. The collection, dedicated to the Belgian royal family, has taken form with the donations made by Belgium's favourite, **King Baudouin**. The royals do not actually live in the adjacent **Palais Royal** – this 19th-century building is more often used for state functions. The family reside in their royal palace in the suburb of Laeken.

Musée de la Dynastie
✉ Hôtel de Bellevue, place des Palais 7, B-1000, Brussels
☎ 02 512 28 21
Fax 02 511 42 53
www.tib.be
10:00–17:00 Tue–Sun
See page 49
Entrance fee, but reductions for groups of more than 20.
Return to the Gare Centrale area of Grand-Place for restaurants and cafés. The museum has a good art shop.
M Trône or Park

Below: *A mounted statue of Godfrey de Bouillon, in front of the church of St Jacques sur Coudenberg, in the Place Royale.*

Musée d'Art Ancien
⊠ Rue de la Régence 3, B-1000, Brussels
☎ 02 508 32 11
02 508 32 32
www.fine-arts-museum.be
info@fine-arts-museum.be
10:00–17:00 Tue–Sun
See page 49
Entrance fee, except on first Wed each month, after 13:00; reduction for groups of over20.
There is a cafeteria within the museum complex and also a good art shop.
M Gare Centrale

See Map C–E5 | ★★★

MUSÉES ROYAUX DES BEAUX-ARTS

This is one of Europe's greatest art collections allow sufficient time to do justice to the many fascinating collections within these two museums.

Musée d'Art Ancien

A bit of a misnomer (for the art comes not from the classical era but from the last five centuries), this museum provides an excellent introduction to the so-called Flemish Primitives (*see* page 12), those ground-breaking painters who revolutionized art by starting the fashion for oil painting back in the early 15th century. There is a good selection of work by such greats as **Rogier van der Weyden**, **Memling**, **Petrus Christus** and **Dierk Bouts**.

A large and well-displayed wing is devoted to the superb painters from the era of Flanders' greatest prosperity. Here is a magnificent collection of works by the trio of fine painters: **Rubens**, **Van Dyck** and **Jordaens**. While many of the canvases will be familiar, there are a number of fascinating oil sketches and many marvellous portraits, not often reproduced in books and posters, by these three talented artists.

Reserve some time to enjoy paintings by 17th-century Italian and French artists, including **Jean-Louis David**, and the realistic scenes in the lobby area, painted by 19th-century **Belgians**.

Below: *A powerful rendition of the Martyrdom of St Peter at the Musée d'Art ancien.*

See Map C–D5 ★★★

Musée d'Art Moderne

Above: *Spacious and well-displayed, the Musée d'Art Moderne has an excellent collection of modern art.*

Instead of rising upwards floor by floor, this extraordinary museum spirals downwards from its neoclassical façade and then spreads out on many different, largely underground floors. An internal well area provides a light source for all the floors. It is connected with the Musée d'Art Ancien by an underground passageway.

This is the address *par excellence* for time out with Belgium's best artists. Look out for Fauvists **Rik Wouters, Jean Brusselmans, Ferdinand Schirren** and **Spilliaert**. Then there are the surrealists: **René Magritte** (for a visit to his house, *see* page 38), **Paul Delvaux** and the German **Max Ernst**, who moved from Dada and made his mark internationally as a surrealist. There are works by expressionists **James Ensor**, half-English but raised in Ostend, and Frenchman **Yves Tanguy** whose work has sometimes been likened to that of Ernst.

The group of abstract Belgian painters (but don't exclude the sculptors) includes **Victor Servranckx** and **Joseph Peeters**, and painters such as Dutchman Karel Appel who formed part of the Cobra Movement. Some of the foreign 19th-century painters whose works are represented include **David, Gauguin, Ingres, Seurat** and **Vuillard**, while 20th-century works include paintings by **Dalí, Allen Jones, Miró** and **Picasso**.

Musée d'Art Moderne
✉ Place Royale 1–2, B-1000, Brussels
☎ 02 508 32 11
📠 02 508 32 32
💻 www.fine-arts-museum.be
✉ info@fine-arts-museum.be
🕒 10:00–17:00 Tue–Sun
🚌 *See* page 49
💰 Entrance fee, except on first Wed each month, after 13:00; reduction for groups of over20.
🍽 Cafeteria within the museum complex and also a good art shop.
M Gare Centrale

Above: *Belgium's most famous comic-strip character, Tintin, accompanied by his indefatigable canine companion, Snowy.*

See Map E–A2 ★★★

CENTRE BELGE DE LA BANDE DESSINÉE

A national institution for the Francophones, this museum dedicated to the **BD** (*Bande Dessinée*), the comic strip, is nevertheless of interest to Anglophones for we have all heard of the **Smurfs** and **Tintin**. The exhibits on how these, and other, famous cartoon characters were produced are totally absorbing.

The museum is located in the beautiful Waucquez warehouse building designed by Art-Nouveau luminary, **Victor Horta**, in 1906. The ground floor (with a great shop, full of ideas for gifts, and a good café) is dedicated to exhibitions, and a revolving show of some of the museum's many original maquettes.

Pride of place goes to **Hergé** (whose real name was Georges Rémy), Belgium's most famous comic-strip master. He rules the roost on the first floor. Here are the drawings, models and machinery that brought the ageless **Tintin** (he debuted in 1929) and his pet dog, **Snowy**, to life for millions of children worldwide. But there are more celebs in this area, including the **Smurfs**, **Le Chat** and **XIII**, and some space is given to the creation of their comic strips. Nearby, there is an exhibition of erotic, moral and humoristic comic strips, and drawings by other notables including **HG Wells** and **Jules Verne**. If you don't find your favourite BD here, have a look at one of the other 40-odd comic shops in Brussels.

Centre Belge de la Bande Dessinée
✉ Anciens Magasins Waucquez, rue des Sables 20, B-1000, Brussels
☎ 02 219 19 80
Fax 02 219 23 76
🕒 10:00–18:00, Tue–Sun
🚌 *See* page 49
💰 Entry fee; reduction for more than 20.
🍽 A pleasant restaurant and a very good art shop.
M Botanique, Gare Centrale or Rogier

See Map E–A3 | ★★

CATHÉDRALE DES SAINT MICHEL ET SAINT GUDULE

The history of this building spans over 1000 years though what we see today is largely the work of 15th-century reconstruction. It is located on a hill which affords fine views of its western façade capped by **Jan van Ruysbroeck**'s Renaissance twin towers. Its patron saints are the archangel St Michel and the rather obscure Ste Gudule, an 11th-century local girl who is recognizable in illustration by the lantern she holds.

Airy, spacious and clean in lines, it is once again the 16th-century **glass windows** which capture the visitor's interest. Coloured light spills through the southern lanterns when the sun illuminates these jewel-like windows, while behind, and over the west door, there is a fine glass ***Last Judgement***.

In the middle of the nave, there is a very ornate Baroque pulpit crafted in oak by **Hendrik Verbruggen** in 1699. It is in total contrast to the simple altar. The **tombs** of Duke John of Brabant and his wife, Margaret of York, are located in the choir, while behind the high altar are the **mausolea** of the Dukes of Brabant and the Archduke of Austria. Note that in the ambulatory there is a small plaque recalling that the famous Flemish artist, **Rogier van der Weyden** (1400–64), was buried in the cathedral. Ancient vestiges of the original church can be visited (a small fee is levied) in the **crypt**, located below the nave.

Cathédrale des St Michel et St Gudule
✉ Place Sainte Gudule, B-1000, Brussels
☎ 02 217 83 45
📠 02 219 96 55
🕒 08:00–18:00, daily
Archaeological remains: same hours Mon–Fri, and 08:30–18:00 Sat and Sun.
Treasury: 10:00–12:00 and 14;00–17:00 Mon–Fri, 10:30–12:30 and 14:00–15:30 Sat, 14:00–17:00 Sun.
Crypt: by appointment only ☎ 02 219 75 30
💰 Entry fee for museums above; cathedral free of charge.
🚌 *See* page 49
🍽 A few cafés and restaurants in the area but a better choice around Grand-Place.
M Gare Centrale

Below: *Renaissance towers crown the cathedral of Saints Michel and Gudule.*

Musée Horta
✉ Rue Américaine 25, B-1060, Brussels
☎ 02 543 04 90
📠 02 538 76 31
💻 www.hortamuseum.be
✉ info@hortamuseum.be
⏱ 14:00–17:30; groups by appointment in mornings.
🚌 Guided tours in English are available by prior written request.
💰 Entry fee, small reduction for pre-booked groups.
🍽 Some cafés nearby, but better to head for Avenue Louise.

See Map D–A3 ★★

MUSÉE HORTA

Although located away from the centre of town, it is definitely worth the journey to see the innovative home of architect and designer **Victor Horta** (1861–1947). A rather sober exterior belies its riotous interior.

The major creator of Art Nouveau, Victor Horta sparked a movement that was to change the face of many a Brussels street (*see* page 48 for more Art-Nouveau buildings), and here in his own home many of his ideas are expounded. Look at those **mirrors**, reflecting through each other into infinity, the coffee-bean **wallpaper**, those extraordinary and graceful scrolls, curves that form lights, lamps, cabinets, door handles, stands and even the stairway which curves around on itself rising to a coloured-glass canopy in the roof. Clever cupboards hide useful space, comfy sofas and beautiful chairs decorate the living rooms, and everywhere glass, steel, ceramic and even terrazzo tiles are used out of their original context to create a stunningly symphonic interior – grand, but full of little surprises. And, best of all, highly functional.

Victor Horta went on to become *the* architect. In the area beyond **Avenue Louise**, around **Vleurgat**, and around the lake at **Ixelles**, his Art-Nouveau buildings have definitely added character to the urban landscape.

Below: *The decorative Art-Nouveau ceiling of Victor Horta's house.*

See Map E–G5 ★★

Below: *Period furniture in the Musée Royaux d'Art et d'Histoire.*

MUSÉE ROYAUX D'ART ET D'HISTOIRE

Do Belgians ever visit museums? The Royal Museum of Art and History must surely have something for everyone, and yet you often have the rooms entirely to yourself. It is housed in a purpose-built palace at the end of **Cinquantenaire Park** and offers visitors classical antiquities, decorative arts, national archaeological exhibits, Medieval treasures, as well as pieces from 'non-European civilizations'. There is also a **Musée pour Aveugles**, containing thoughtfully staged exhibits for the visually handicapped.

The archaelogical finds on Belgian soil are limited and displayed in various dioramas. The **classical exhibits** are beautifully arranged (check out those Egyptian mummies and their mummified animals), with much space devoted to the **Greeks** and the **Roman** empire. Fabulous collections of **furniture** and **ceramics** fill large halls in the decorative arts section, while the small but stunning (recently revamped with great lighting) **Salle au Trésor** holds some magnificent religious works. There is another superb department with **Art-Deco glass**, **tapestries** and **ceramics**. Unfortunately because of its size and the lack of staff, not all the sections are open at the same time.

Musée Royaux d'Art et d'Histoire
Parc du Cinquantenaire 10, B-1000, Brussels
02 741 72 11
02 733 77 35
www.kmkg-mrah.be
info@kmkg-mrah.be
Museum: 09:30–17:00 Tue–Fri, 10:00–17:00 Sat and Sun, Treasure room: 10:00–12:00 and 13:00–16:00 daily
Entry fee; free first Wed afternoon of the month.
Free tours by appointment only.
A good cafeteria and excellent art shop.
M Merode or Schuman

See Map E–G5 ★★

Above: *The vast exhibition space at Autoworld houses a world-class collection of cars and utilitarian vehicles.*

AUTOWORLD

This hangar-like building occupies a purpose-built space, constructed to house the prestigious **Salon de l'Auto** from 1902–34. With over 400 vehicles in perfect working order, it is a car-lover's haven and many make it the only stop on a brief tour of Brussels.

Interestingly, Belgium was creating cars while many nations were still toying with bikes. Belgian brands such as the **Minerva Imperia**, **Germain** and **Vivinus** motors bear witness to this industrious era between World Wars. The collection of motors (including an ancient fire engine and President Kennedy's 1963 Berlin car) is one of the finest in Europe and traces the history of the motor car from its first efforts in 1886 up to the present day. Look out for those shiny black Citroëns, the Bugatti, Bentley and Mercedes, Citroën 2CV and the early Beetle. Although there is a cafeteria, the museum could do with some benches.

Autoworld
⊠ Parc du Cinquantenaire 11, B-1000, Brussels
☎ 02 736 41 65
Fax 02 736 51 36
www.autoworld.be
autoworld@skynet.be
10:00–17:00 winter, 10:00–18:00 summer.
Entry fee; reductions for groups.
Guided tours upon written request.
Cafeteria and shop.
M Schuman or Merode

See Map D–D5,D6 ★★

BOIS DE LA CAMBRE

One of the pleasures of Brussels is that the city encompasses some delightful park areas, many of which were formerly beyond the suburbs in the countryside. The 124ha (50-acre) Bois de la Cambre, in which lies the **Abbaye de la Cambre**, is one such area and offers a peaceful retreat from the commerce of nearby Avenue Louise and Chaussée de Vleurgat, not to forget the embassy-trimmed Avenue Franklin Roosevelt. The woods used to be part of the vast **Forêt de Soignes** (*see* page 32) but it was annexed to the town in 1842 and, in part, relandscaped by landscape artist, **Edouard Keilig**. The beautiful deciduous trees part to reveal a boating lake, semi-formal, tiered gardens and the **Théâtre de Poche**.

The abbey was founded in 1201 by a Belgian noblewoman who gave it to the Citeaux Order. The abbey buildings suffered during the Wars of Religion and were rebuilt twice, in the 16th and 18th centuries. Parts of the church, however, survived and remain as the only 14th-century part of the complex. Rimming two quadrangles, the abbey buildings today house the Belgian Geographical Institute and La Cambre Art School.

Abbaye de la Cambre
✉ Bave Emile Duray 11, B-1000, Brussels (access by bus).
☎ 022 648 11 21
🕒 09:00–12:00, 15:00–18:30 Mon–Fri, 15:00–18:00 Sat, and 08:00–12:30, 15:00–18:00 Sun.
💰 Free entry.
🍽 Return to Avenue Louise for a good selection of cafés and restaurants.

Below: *The façade of the large Abbaye de la Cambre, between Ixelles and Uccle.*

See Map A–C2,D2 ★

FORÊT DE SOIGNES

Vast and beautiful, the Soignes Forest is just to the south of Brussels – a wonderfully bucolic area yet so conveniently near the city centre that it is a favourite for well-heeled commuters and the location of foreign embassies.

Within this forested area is the satellite town of **Tervuren** with its attractive lakes, ponds and beautiful parks. On its outskirts is the massive museum (*see* below) dedicated to the culture of Central Africa.

Musée Royal de l'Afrique Centrale
✉ chaussee de Louvaine 13, B-3080
☎ 02 769 52 11
💻 www.lafricamuseum.be
🕒 11:00–17:00 Tue–Fri and 10:00–18:00 Sat and Sun
💰 Entry fee; reduction for groups.
🚌 Guided tours by written request, three weeks in advance.
🍴 A fun cafeteria.

Musée Royal de l'Afrique Centrale

This is a purpose-built space created in 1879 by **King Leopold II** as part of an exhibition on the Congo – which, at that time, formed part of his possessions. Such was the success of the show that the Royal Museum of Central Africa has remained intact – in some cases to its dusty detriment. However, it has a fascinating collection of items (ideal for children) including a vast taxidermy section of stuffed animals, various diaramas containing birds in representations of their natural habitats, the usual elephant skeletons, a fine selection of colourful (and often fearsome) ethnic masks, wooden sculpture and decorative dress. A well-designed section shows the disastrous effects of tropical rainfall after deforestation.

Opposite: *The fields of Waterloo form a bucolic foil for the hill known as the Butte du Lion.*
Below: *Musée Royal de l'Afrique Centrale houses many items from what was once known as Belgian Congo.*

See Map A–C3 | ★

WATERLOO

Once the site of a disastous battle, now a calm sea of green crops, Waterloo is a must for the historians. On 18 June 1815, Prussian **Marshal Blücher** and the **Duke of Wellington**, heading the Anglo-Dutch-German alliance, met the more numerous French forces lead by **Napoleon** (*see* page 8) for a short but decisive 10-hour battle. Napoleon had danced the previous night away and had foolishly postponed an attack the following morning because the continuous summer rains had churned the ground to a quagmire. By evening 13,000 were dead, 35,000 were injured and Napoleon was, more or less, on his way to exile on the remote island of St Helena. How warfare has changed!

The town of Waterloo breathes battle memorabilia. The Duke of Wellington's Headquarters are now the **Wellington Museum**, while **Napoleon's Last Headquarters** are also open to visits. A Waxwork Museum brings the different personages and battalions to life, and most visitors drive out to the **Butte du Lion**, the conical Lion's Hill which overlooks the battlefields and where there is a visitor centre.

Every five years the **Battle of Waterloo** is re-enacted by a (voluntary) cast of 2000 'soldiers' creating a colourful and memorable spectacle.

Wellington Museum
✉ chaussée de Bruxelles 147, 1410
☎ 02 354 78 06
Fax 02 354 28 31
www. museewellington.com
museewellington@ museewellington.com
09:30–18:30 summer and 10:30–17:00 winter.
Entry fee.
Tours by written request, 10 days' notice.
Cafés and restaurants along main street.

Napoleon's Last Headquarters
✉ Chaussée de Bruxelles 66, 1472 Vieux Genappe
☎ 02 384 24 24
dernier.qg.napoleon @belgacom.net
10:00–18:30 summer and 13:00–17:00 winter.

Butte du Lion Centre
09:30–18:30 summer and 10:30–16:00 winter.

Chocolate
Theobroma cacao, the cocoa tree, is a tropical plant native to Mexico. It produces a pod full of white, unpleasant-tasting beans. However, fermented and dry-roasted they change into the raw material of chocolate. This can be separated into **cocoa butter** and **cocoa solids**. With the addition of sugar (sometimes milk) and a small percentage of vegetable oils, and treated by a process called **conching** which heats, cools and rolls the produce into a smooth blend of ingredients, chocolate as we know it is formed. Some 7000 people in Belgium are employed in the luxury chocolate industry.

The world's biggest producer of chocolate beans is the Ivory Coast, followed by Ghana, Indonesia, Brazil, Niger, Cameroon and Malaysia. Some 2,800,000 tons of beans are produced annually.

Churches

Saint Nicolas

A plain western façade hides the dark, mysterious interior of this church, dedicated to Saint Nicolas, the patron saint of merchants. It has a crooked nave and a distinct Eastern flavour and is Brussels' oldest church, having been founded in the 11th century. A (very) small *Madonna and Child* is attributed to Rubens.

✉ *rue au Beurre 1,*
☎ *02 513 80 22,*
⌚ *07:30–18:30 Mon–Fri, 09:00–18:00 Sat–Sun,*
M *Bourse.*

Église Sainte Catherine

Sadly, this neo-Gothic church, in a slightly seedy neighbourhood, suffered a serious fire and, having been doused with water, it is still 'drying out'. It has an airy, spacious interior, designed in 1854 by **Joseph Poelaert**.

✉ *Place Ste Catherine,*
☎ *02 513 34 81,*
⌚ *08:30–17:00 Mon–Sat, 09:00–12:00 Sun,*
M *Ste Catherine.*

Nôtre-Dame de la Chapelle

The first religious building on the site dates back to the 12th century, though much of what one sees today is from the 14th–17th centuries.

✉ *Place de la Chapelle,*
☎ *02 512 07 37,*
⌚ *09:00–16:00 daily in summer, 12:00–16:00 daily in winter,*
M *Gare Centrale.*

Interesting Buildings

La Bourse

This elegant and classically-inspired Stock Exchange building was designed in 1873 by **Léon Suys**.

✉ *rue H. Maus 2,*
⌚ *not open to public,*
M *Bourse.*

Théâtre Royale de la Monnaie

Another **Poelaert** building. The architect rebuilt it in 1855 and it was renovated to its

present, attractive form in the 1980s.

⊠ *Place de la Monnaie, rue Léopold 4,*
☎ *02 229 12 11,*
⏲ *11:00–18:00 Tue–Sat,*
M *De Brouckère.*

European Parliament

Located in the Quartier Leopold, behind the station, is the steel and glass European Parliament which opened in 1998. The westward side of the pleasant, tree-filled **Parc Leopold** is full of glitzy, expensive buildings and Eurocrats. The once imposing **Berlaymont** building was formerly the Commission headquarters – until the percentage of asbestos used in its construction was revealed. It is currently undergoing serious asbestos-removing renovations.

⊠ *Rue Wiertz,*
☎ *02 512 07 37,*
⏲ *audio-guided visits at 10:00 and 15:00,*
M *Maalbeek, Schuman.*

Museums

Musée du Cacao et du Chocolat

This small, interesting museum, right on the Grand-Place, documents the cultivation of cocoa beans worldwide, and demonstrates how chocolate is produced.

⊠ *Grand-Place 13,*
☎ *02 514 20 48,*
📠 *02 514 52 05,*
💻 *www.mucc.be*
⏲ *10:00–16:30 Tue–Sun, but daily in July and August,*
M *Bourse, Gare Centrale.*

Musée de la Brasserie

From humble beginnings in the 18th century to high-tech

Revolution was Born

The **Théâtre Royale de la Monnaie** has a claim to fame that transcends its architecture. In 1830 the Belgian revolution started outside the theatre. The theatre-going audience, roused by patriotic music, streamed out and joined the revolutionaries. After driving out the Dutch they established the first monarchy under a Belgian king.

Opposite: *The European Parliament will soon represent some 20 different countries.*
Below: *Demonstration of praline manufacture in the Chocolate Museum.*

Jacques Brel (1929–1978)

Poet and songwriter Jacques Brel had a short, but prolific life and was a major player in the world of 20th-century French song.

He was born in Brussels but set off for Paris, aged 24, armed with songs and a guitar. He worked his way through cabarets, graduating onto the stage at Paris' Olympia and Bobino theatres. He toured much of the world and had considerable success in the United States.

In the 1970s he discovered the beauty of Polynesia and moved to the Marquesas islands but it was for just two years. In 1978 he died of lung cancer.

Brel's best-known songs include: *Ne me quitte pas*, *Quand on n'a que l'amour*, *Les bonbons*, *J'arrive*, and *Amsterdam*.

production in the 21st, the visitor can see the workings of a brewery. Its detractors say that the **Musée Bruxellois de la Gueuze** in Anderlecht is a far superior place to learn about beer, and the tasting is excellent.

Musée de la Brasserie
✉ *Grand-Place 10,*
☎ *02 511 49 87,*
📠 *02 511 32 59,*
💻 *www.beerparadise.be*
🕒 *10:00–17:00 daily,*
M *Bourse, Gare Centrale.*

Musée Bruxellois de la Gueuze
✉ *rue Gheude 56, B-1070, Brussels,*
☎ *02 521 49 28,*
🕒 *09:00–17:00 Mon–Fri, 10:00–17:00 Sat,*
M *Gare du Midi, Clemenceau.*

Mont des Arts

The sloping land between the Lower and Upper Town has been landscaped into an interesting 'bridge' between the two areas and is decorated with sculpture and a small garden. It is illuminated at night.

✉ *Rue Montagne de la Cour,*
🕒 *24 hours,*
M *Gare Centrale.*

Musée des Instruments de Musique (MIM)

This museum is housed in the **Old England** building. Once a smart store, this unusual but attractive black-coloured, four-storey Art-Nouveau building has been carefully renovated to accommodate the museum. Exhibits include more than 1500 musical instruments – not just visual exhibits but aural too. A real find for music lovers.

✉ *rue Montagne de la Cour 2,*
☎ *02 545 01 30,*
📠 *02 545 01 77,*
💻 *www.mim.fgov.be*
🕒 *10:00–16:30,*
M *Parc.*

Fondation Internationale Jacques Brel

One of the 1960s greats in the French poetry in song genre, **Jacques Brel** (1929–78) was born in Brussels. This foundation is dedicated to the Belgian singer-songwriter and, with 3-D sound and light projections, personal items and recorded reflections and songs, Brel explains himself.

✉ *Place de la Vielle Halle aux Blés,*
☎ *02 511 10 20,*
📠 *02 511 10 21,*
💻 *www.jacquesbrel.be*
🕒 *11:00–18:00 Tue–Sat,*
M *Gare Centrale.*

Musée de la Dynastie

This museum, covering the Belgian royal dynasty and a memorial to King Baudouin, is located in the elegant **Hôtel de Bellevue**. The exhibits (busts, furniture, books, documents and photos) mark the passage of each reign in a chronological order and outline many aspects of monarchical duties. The well-proportioned, cream-coloured mansion itself has been beautifully maintained.

✉ *Hôtel de Bellevue, place des Palais 7,*
☎ *02 512 28 21,*
📠 *02 511 42 53,*
🕒 *10:00–17:00 Tue–Sun,*
M *Parc, Trône.*

Muséum des Sciences Naturelles

This is a huge exhibit – and a favourite with children. Bits of bone, feathers, skins and skeletons trace the evolution of species and include a number of impressive dinosaur remains. Among the most memorable exhibits are the whales (just look at that blue whale!) and the fine display of minerals.

NATO

In addition to the government of the country, Brussels is the seat of NATO, the **North Atlantic Treaty Organization**, which has gained rather more importance in the last few years than in the previous ones. Since 1992, Brussels has become the capital of Europe and provides headquarters to various organizations of the European Union, including the **European Parliament**, resulting in a large influx of diplomats and personnel in the last decade.

Opposite: *The International Jacques Brel Foundation is dedicated to Brussels-born Brel, songwriter and poet.*
Below: *A delightful Art-Nouveau building, Old England houses the Musée des Instruments de Musique.*

Above: *The Salle au Trésors, Musée Royaux d'Art et d'Histoire* (see *page 29*), *exhibits some superb Medieval sculptures and relics.*

Museums
On the first Wednesday of the month, some museums are open free of charge in the afternoon. Many museums offer guided tours on written request. Practically all museums have wheelchair access – but check with the individual museum for exact details prior to visiting.

✉ *rue Vautier 29,*
☎ *02 627 42 38,*
📠 *02 627 41 13,*
💻 *www. sciencesnaturelles.be*
🕒 *09:30–16:45 Tue–Fri, 10:00–18:00 weekends. Closed major public holidays,*
M *Maelbeek.*

Bruxella 1238

This underground museum is, for archaeology buffs, worth visiting on the weekly guided tour. Here are the remains (including stonework, ceramics and bone relics) of an early Brussels convent (hence the date) discovered when recent digging work was in progress.

✉ *Rue de la Bourse,*
☎ *02 279 43 50,*
📠 *02 279 43 62,*
🕒 *Wed. 10:15 in English; 11:15 in French,*
M *Bourse, De Brouckère.*

Musée Royal de l'Armee et d'Histoire Militaire

One of the largest military museums, the exhibition presents a collection of ancient arms and armoury, the different Belgian armies, the evolution of modern warfare, and a section devoted to military air power.

✉ *Parc du Cinquantenaire 3,*
☎ *02 737 78 11,*
📠 *02 737 78 02,*
💻 *www.klm-mra.be*
🕒 *09:00–12:00, 13:00–16:30 Tue–Sun,*
M *Schuman, Merode.*

Musée René Magritte

This small brick house was where the surrealist artist Magritte (1898–1967) lived and worked between 1930 and 1954 (*see also* page 25). Discover his humble living room, studio, garden, bedroom and various letters, drawings and works painted, or acquired, by the artist.

✉ *rue Esseghem 135,*
☎ *02 428 26 26,*
📠 *02 428 26 26,*
🕒 *10:00–18:00 Wed–Sun,*
💻 *www. magrittemuseum.be*
M *Belgica, Bockstael.*

Musée David et Alice van Buuren

This art collection belonged to the wealthy Dutch van Buuren couple and its star items (ivories, ceramics and their superb collection of European paintings) make the journey to Uccle worthwhile.

⊠ *avenue L Errera 41,*
☎ *02 343 48 51,*
℻ *02 347 66 89,*
💻 *www.museumvan-buuren.com*
◷ *13:00–18:00, 14:00–18:00 Mon, gardens 14:00–17:30,*
🚌 *trams 23, 90, buses 38, 60.*

Maison d'Erasme

This (now suburban) house was built as a guesthouse for the chapter of Anderlecht, and was also where Erasmus (1469–1536) recuperated from illness in 1521. Today it holds an interesting collection of books, documents and is period furnished.

⊠ *rue du Chapitre 31,*
☎ *02 521 13 83,*
℻ *02 527 12 69,*
◷ *10:00–17:00 Tue–Sun,*
M *St Guidon.*

Parks and Gardens

Parc de Bruxelles

This semi-formal shady park (once a hunting lodge) opposite the Palais Royal, with its statues and fountains, is a pleasant place to stroll or picnic.

⊠ *Place des Palais,*
◷ *06:00–21:00,*
M *Parc.*

Jardin Botanique

Highlight of this garden is its ancient chateau, rebuilt for Charlotte, the ex-empress of Mexico. The gardens have a good glasshouse and medicinal herbs.

⊠ *Domaine de Bouchout, Meise,*
☎ *02 260 09 70,*
℻ *02 260 09 47,*
◷ *09:00–17:00 daily,*
M *Botanique.*

Jardins d'Egmont

This garden brings some green to a densely urban area and is a popular

Petit Sablon

Up to the late 19th century, the Place du Petit Sablon was a cemetery where the ex-patients of the nearby Hospital of Saint Jean were interred. In 1890 it opened as a public garden, designed by **H Beyaert** who was, it is said, inspired by the fence that surrounded the pools at the former ducal palace at Coudenberg. **A C Fraikin's** imposing statue of the counts of Egmont and Hornes was commissioned in 1864 to commemorate the spot where the two counts were beheaded, but it was later moved to its present position in the Place du Petit Sablon.

Below: *Graced by many sculptures and ponds, the Parc de Bruxelles is one of central Brussels' largest parks.*

More Parks
For those with more time and a desire to go further afield, the **Forêt de Soignes** (*see* page 32) is a wonderful wooded area of walking trails, lakes and semi-formal gardens extending through to **Tervuren** where the Musée Royal de l'Afrique Centrale is located in fine semi-formal parkland.

The **Bois de la Cambre** (*see* page 31) is also a pleasant alternative to the city centre.

In **Ixelles**, the *étangs* (ponds) bring a bit of rural tranquillity into the urban panorama.

Further afield the **Parc de Wolvendael**, in the suburb of Uccle, has a delightful 17th-century pavilion and is surrounded by lovely parkland.

place for picnic lunches. It's also known for its well.

✉ *Blvd Waterloo or Rue aux Laines,*
⏲ *06:00–21:00,*
M *Louise.*

Parc Leopold

In the European section of Brussels. *See* page 35.

Parc du Cinquantenaire

In European Brussels, this large park with its grandiose 1880-built triumphal arch is a beautiful mix of established trees and grassy lawns. *See* pages 29 and 30 for details of its museums. A small neoclassical temple (rarely open but you can peer through the cracks) designed by Victor Horta stands in one corner near the large mosque.

Below: *The 1880 triumphal arch marks the start of the Parc du Cinquantenaire.*

Parc de Laeken

This is the leafy, park-filled suburb in which the royals now live. Their magnificent greenhouses are only open to the public briefly in May. However, the park area has been developed for tourism and at its northern extremes there is a large exhibition centre. In its midst lies the **Tour Japonaise** and a Japanese garden, a delightful addition to the tree-filled landscape. Nearby, the **Pavillon Chinois** (Chinese Pavilion) has a good collection of porcelain. In Heysel, the odd **Atomium** (a gigantic iron molecule fashioned from aluminium and steel, and housing temporary exhibtions) stands amid a large avenue, while **Mini-Europe** (*see* page 43) is a popular venue for children.

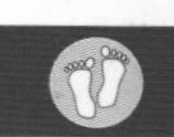

ACTIVITIES

Sport and Recreation

With beautiful (and easily accessible) parks and forests around the city, sporting options for the visitor mainly include **walking**, **cycling** and **jogging**. Most clubs in town require membership, so for short-term travellers they are not an option.

But the Belgians are cyclists – remember Eddy Merckx? There is an annual **Grand Prix** named after him. So, if you're planning on bringing your bicycle, you'll be welcome to use the tracks through greater Brussels and enjoy the forest trails. Alternatively, you can hire bikes at **Pro-Vélo**, ✉ rue de Londres 15, Ixelles, ☎ 02 502 73 55, 💻 www.provelo.org 🖱 provelo@skynet.be

Golfing visitors can play at courses in Waterloo, Anderlecht, La Hulpe or Duisburg. For details and fees contact the **Fédération royale Belge de Golf**, ✉ chaussée de la Hulpe 110, ☎ 02 672 23 89.

Unusual Exhibitions

Espace Photographique Contretype
Creative photos.
✉ avenue de la Jonction 1, B-1060, Brussels
☎ 02 538 42 20
🖱 contrety@hebel.net
🕒 13:00–18:00 Tue–Sun

Centre culturel Art media
Temporary exhibitions in a 1925 mansion.
✉ rue Defacqz 14, B-1050, Brussels
☎ 02 544 08 33

Flagey
Radio studios and concert venue.
✉ Place Sainte Croix, B-1050, Brussels
☎ 02 627 16 40
🖱 sa.flagey@skynet.be
🕒 daily

Alternative Brussels

The gay community in Brussels is growing and it also has a number of sympathetic venues. These include a handful of bars such as **Le Belgica** (an old-fashioned place

Below: *The pretty landscaped lakes at Ixelles provide a place for a quiet moment and even tempt local anglers.*

Scientastique Museum
✉ Station Métro Bourse (1st level)
☎ 02 732 13 36
Fax 02 736 53 35
www.scientastic.be
scientastic@yahoo.fr
⌚ 14:00–17:30 weekends and school holidays, 12:30–14:00 term time.
discount for groups of over 25 persons.
cafeteria
M Bourse

Aqualibi
✉ rue Joseph Deschamps 9, 1300 Wavre.

Océade
✉ Bruparck B1020
☎ 02 478 43 20
Fax 02 478 00 90
www.oceade.be
info@oceade.be
⌚ 10:00–22:00 daily, Apr–Sep.
cafeteria

which pulls in the crowds), **Le Duquesnoy** (raunchy and a bit borderline but with a certain success) and **Tels Quels** (catering for the lesbian and gay community). Gay associations and helplines include the **English-Speaking Gay Group** (good for long-term newcomers wanting to make acquaintances) and **Tel'Egal**. For details, *see* panel on page 71.

Fun for Children

There are plenty of easily accessible things to amuse the younger generation in and around Brussels.

The **Scientastique Museum** is designed to make science friendly. It is a hands-on affair where children can change the perceptions of their senses with amusing experiments such as changing their appearances with mirrors and warping their voices.

Aqualibi water park recreates the tropics with its balmy heat. Slides, waves, jacuzzis and waterfalls make this play area a real

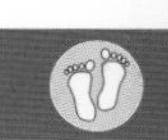

hit. It is within the Walibi theme park, at Wavre – about 25km (16 miles) from the centre of Brussels on the E411 in the direction of Namur. More water fun is available at **Océade** (*see* opposite side panel).

Puppet theatres are always popular and although the puppets speak French or Flemish, actions generally speak louder than words. Try **Le Peruchet**, where puppet performances are staged thrice weekly and a museum houses over 4000 marionettes.

There is plenty to see and do at **Mini-Europe**. The leaning tower of Pisa, Big Ben, the Grand-Place, canals of Venice and even the Arc de Triomphe are there and little more than the height of an adult. Children can cause Vesuvius to erupt or run a *corrida* (bullfight) in Seville. Spend a good part of the day here so as to benefit from its many exhibits and its reasonable entrance fee.

Musée Royal de l'Afrique Centrale, a huge museum in fine parkland, appeals to adults and children (*see* page 32). Perhaps take a picnic or eat at the Simba cafeteria.

Another easy museum for children to get to grips with is the **Muséum des Sciences Naturelles** (*see* page 37).

Walking Tours

Walking Historic Brussels

A good tour of the centre takes around two hours, without stops, though it is pleasant to take slightly longer. Plan to do this in the morning or afternoon and break for a bite or drink along the route.

Heading southward from **Grand-Place** (map C–4C) via Rue de Buls, notice on the left of the road a fine Art-Noveau plaque (*see* page 13), by Victor Rousseau dedicated

Le Peruchet
✉ Musée International de la Marionnette, ave de la Forêt 50, B-1050
☎ 02 673 87 30
🕒 15:00 Wed, Sat and Sun, closed Jul and Aug.

Mini-Europe
✉ Bruparck
☎ 02 474 13 13
📠 02 478 26 75
💻 www.minieurope.com
✉ info@minieurope.com
🕒 09:30–17:00 Easter to early January and open 09:30–23:00 Fri, Sat and Sun evenings, mid-July to mid-August.
💰 dicount for groups of over 20 persons.
🍽 restaurant and cafeteria
M Heysel

Opposite: *The Chinese festival is just one of Brussels' many festivals that will appeal to children.*

Main Buildings on the Grand-Place
Nº 1 La Maison des Boulangers; bakers' guildhouse.
Nº 2–3 La Brouette; tallow merchants.
Nº 4 Le Sac; coopers.
Nº 5 La Louve; the archers.
Nº 6 Maison du Cornet; ferrymen.
Nº 7 Maison du Renard; haberdashers.
Nº 8 L'Étoile; court sentencer.
Nº 9 Maison du Cygne; butchers.
Nº 10 L'Arbre d'Or; brewers.
Nº 11–12 private houses.
Nº 13–19 Maison des Ducs de Brabant.
Nº 20 Le Cerf, private house.
Nº 23 L'Ange.
Nº 24 La Chaloupe d'Or; tailors.
Nº 26–27 Le Pigeon; painters.
Nº 28 La Chambrette d'Amman.
La Maison du Roi.
Nº 34 La Heaume.
Nº 35 Le Paon.
Nº 36–37 Le Petit Renard et le Chêne.
Nº 38–39 Ste Barbe et l'Ane.

Opposite: *Designed in 1783 by French architect Barnabé Guimard, the Palais de la Nation houses the country's parliament.*

to **Charles Buls**, one-time mayor of Brussels, from the merchants of the city. Continue on down Rue de l'Etuve and you'll see people milling on the corner of this road and the Rue du Chêne. This is where the **Manneken Pis** draws the crowds (*see* page 19 for more details). Head uphill from the architecturally pleasant Rue du Chêne to the Place de la Vielle Halle aux Blés where, on the left, the **Fondation Internationale Jacques Brel** (*see* page 37) is located. From here the architecture takes a dive. Walk along Rue de l'Escalier, crossing the Boulevard de l'Empereur, and there in front, incongruously overshadowed by a bowling alley, is the **Tour Anneessens**, a remnant of the 12th-century city fortifications.

From this tower, take the Rue de Rollebeek toward the **Place du Grand Sablon** (*see* page 20) and walk slowly up this elegant square to the **Place du Petit Sablon**. The church on your left is **Nôtre-Dame du Sablon** (*see* page 22). The busy street which divides the two squares and runs along the side of this elegant church is Rue de la Régence, leading eastward past the **Musées Royaux des Beaux-Arts** (*see* page 24) into the **Place Royale**. An equestrian statue of crusader **Godfrey de Bouillon** now graces the centre of the square (*see* page 23) which has, on its east side, the classically inspired **church of St Jacques sur Coudenberg** (*see* page 23).

Ahead lies the **Parc de Bruxelles** (map E–B4) and on your right, as you enter the Place des Palais, the **Hôtel de Bellevue** with the **Dynasty Museum** (*see* page 37) and the **Royal Palace** (*see* page 23). The park is a great place to relax. There are statues,

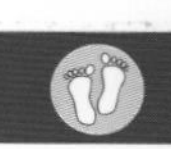

fountains, ponds and shady spots. At its northern end lies the **Palais de la Nation**, Belgium's very elegant Parliament building. Turn west here and head back into the old town, via Rue de la Loi, and then right into Rue de la Chancellerie, to the **Cathedral** (*see* page 27) on **Place Sainte Gudule**. Note the statue of King Leopold in the gardens below the cathedral. Turning northwards along Rue d'Assaut, then Rue du Marais, you'll come to a seedy part of town. Take the small street poetically named Persil (parsley) and you'll see the **Place des Martyrs** (map C, D2) just ahead. Once an elegant square, today it is the hangout of modern martyrs with political grievances. In its midst are four low-relief sculptures in classical style, relating the 1830 revolution against the Dutch. Those who lost their lives in the uprising, which started just a block away, are buried here.

The Old City
Old Brussels was surrounded by 400m (440yd) of sandstone walls at the end of the 11th and early 12th century. These used to have 50 different defence towers and seven gates. Tour Anneessens is one of the last remaining towers.

Walking Historic Brussels
Location: Map C–4C
Distance: approx 4km (2.5miles)
Duration: 2–3 hours
Start: Grand-Place
Finish: Grand-Place
There are plenty of restaurants in and around Grand-Place.

Above: *The façade of Léon Suys' Stock Exchange, designed in 1873.*

By walking a few metres down Rue St Michel and then left via **Rue Neuve**, you will reach the popular shopping street, **Place de la Monnaie.** It was here that that patriotism wrung the hearts of the Bruxellois at the **Théâtre Royale de la Monnaie** and the revolution took shape (*see* panel page 35). Turn southwards along the Rue des Fripiers towards Rue du Midi, and you'll find **La Bourse**, the city's imposing **Stock Exchange** (*see* page 34) on your right, and under it, the museum **Bruxella 1238** (*see* page 38). From here, stop a moment to look inside the **church of St Nicolas** (*see* page 34), before headng back along Rue au Beurre to the Grand-Place.

Walking Tour of Sainte Catherine

A second, shorter walk, one less frequented by tourists, takes you through another historic area of Brussels.

From the Grand-Place, walk westward past the Stock Exchange and cross the busy Boulevard Anspach, then stroll along Rue Devaux (map C–C3), with its many Asian restaurants, until it becomes **Rue Ste Catherine**. This runs into the slightly seedy square of the same name, a wide open place with an excellent daily produce **market** (*see* page 21) and some good and inexpensive restaurants. The **church of Ste Catherine** (*see* page 34) was once a beautiful building, but is now one which sorely needs renovation. From here walk up the

Walking Tour of Sainte Catherine
Location: Map C–4C
Distance: 2.5km (1.5 miles)
Duration: 2 hours
Start: Grand-Place
Finish: Place St Géry.
Plenty of restaurants around Ste Catherine and Place St Géry.

Quai au Bois à Bruler, a large, long and thin square, today paved and with fountains, though once it was the water-filled docks for unloading firewood. The other side, lined with 19th-century buildings, is called the Quai aux Briques, again after its canal-borne merchandise. This is another top-class area for seafood and inexpensive yet good restaurants.

Halfway up the Quai au Bois à Bruler take the residential Rue du Peuplier which runs into the rather run-down **Place du Béguinage** with, in its centre, the fine Baroque façade of the **church of St Jean Baptiste au Béguinage**, ◷ 10:00–17:00 daily, built by L Fayd'Herbe in 1657. Beyond the church, via Rue de l'Infirmerie, lies the huge **Hospice Pacheco**, built between 1824 and 1827 and now a state-of-the-art geriatric institute (not open to the public). The western end of the Rue du Grand Hospice runs back into the Quai au Bois à Bruler.

You might retrace your steps here to the other side of the square and then branch off after Place Ste Catherine to the Rue du Vieux Marché aux Grains, the old corn market of yore, and then down left on Rue Antoine Dansaert (the city's fashion capital) which brings you to the **Place St Géry**. This was believed to be the island site where St Géry founded a chapel in the 6th century. It's better known now for evening entertainment (*see* page 70).

Béguinages

These shelters were founded for single woman who elected to live quasi-nun-like lives, without taking formal orders. They nursed the sick and cared for bereaved families. Although they were Protestant and found throughout northern Europe, they all but disappeared during the Reformation but survived, even thrived, in Flanders. All that remains of this Béguinage in Brussels is its church.

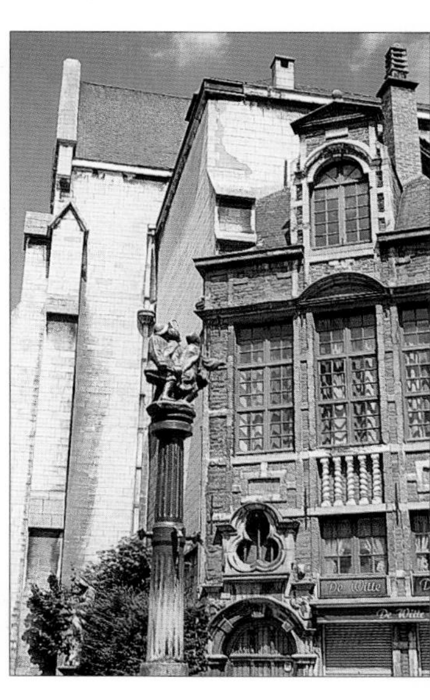

Below: *Founded in the 11th century, the church of St Nicholas is Brussels' oldest church.*

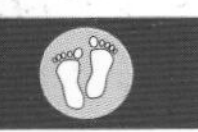

Discovering Subway Art

Odd though it may be, Brussels has a lot of art in or at the entrances of its subway stations. This too provides a theme for a morning's excursion. An inexpensive day-long subway ticket means that you can visit a number of stations and see the works of art (by artists such as **Paul Delvaux**), which range from paintings and tilework to sculpture. The Tourist Office produces a booklet with a listing of all subway art.

In Pursuit of Art Nouveau

Brussels proclaims itself as the Art Nouveau capital and indeed, from 1894–1905, it decorated its urban landscape with an innovative series of houses, factories and mansions. Wander around two major areas of Brussels (the Upper and Lower Town, and the Ixelles, Avenue Louise area) and enjoy the eccentricity.

At the bottom of Rue de l'Etuve, on rue du Lombard 30–32 (map C–C4), **Paul Vizzanova** built a fine house. **Victor Horta** was responsible for the **Hôtel Frison**, on rue Lebeau 37, just to the south of Place de la Justice. On rue Montagne de la Cour 2 stands **Old England** (*see* page 36), the store designed in 1899 by Paul Saintenoy. The **Palais des Beaux-Arts** (Map C–E5) was also a Horta-designed building, as was the building which now houses the **Centre Belge de la Bande Dessinée** (*see* page 26). More Horta façades can be seen in the rue de l'Evêque 5, and rue Grétry 18.

Head back to the Stock Exchange and, at rue de la Bourse 18, stop at **Café Cirio** (*see* panel, page 52) for a drink – it's pure Art

Opposite: *Bus tours take in most of Brussels and travel to the country's popular tourist destinations.*
Right: *Modern art brightens up the subway system.*

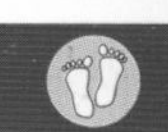

Nouveau, as is its competition, **Le Falstaff**, a 1900 tavern on the other side of the Stock Exchange. Then spare a few minutes to walk up to the renovated **Hotel Métropole**, Place de Brouckère, where flamboyance, Art Deco and Art Nouveau all collide.

The area around Ixelles is full of pleasant homes. You could visit **Victor Horta's** house (*see* page 28), wander around the Ixelles lakes where architect **Ernest Blérot** built a large number of houses and check out those in Rue Faider. Other Horta buildings in Ixelles include the **Hôtel Solvay**, ave Louise 224, **Hôtel Max Hallet**, ave Louise 346, **Hôtel Tassel**, rue Janson 6, and **Sander Pierron** house, rue de Aqueduc 157.

Organized Tours

For a quick tour of Brussels, head for an organized tour. Various hop-on, hop-off buses with multi-language commentaries delivered through headphones give a good do-it-yourself tour. Otherwise try one of the companies listed in the side panel.

Organized Tours

Pro Velo
Organized cycle tours of the capital.
✉ rue de Londres 15, B-1050
☎ 02 502 73 55

De Boeck's Sightseeing Tours
Bus tours of the capital, and other cities, start from Grand-Place.
✉ Rue de la Colline, B-1000
☎ 02 513 77 44

Guides TIB-GBB
Guided, themed and individual tours.
✉ Hôtel de Ville, Grand-Place, B-1000
☎ 02 548 04 48

Arcadia
For walking tours and bus tours with specialist themes.
✉ Rue du Métail, St Gilles, B-1060
☎ 02 534 38 19

Best Shopping Areas
- **Galeries Saint Hubert** (map C–D3/4) for chic boutiques and people-watching.
- **Rue Antoine Dansaert** (map C–B3) for contemporary fashion.
- **Place du Grand Sablon** (map C–D6) for boutiques, antiques and chocolates.
- **Avenue Louise** (map D–B2,C3) for international high fashion and accessories.
- **Rue Neuve** (map C–D2) for chain-store fashion.
- **Museum shops** in the Musées Royaux des Beaux-Arts (*see* page 24), and Musée Royaux d'Art et d'Histoire (*see* page 29).
- **Sainte Catherine** (map C–A2) for luxury food produce (and good meals in between shopping).

Shops

Brussels's best shopping is either in the Lower Town, or around the Avenue Louise to Ixelles area. Designer shops are in the Avenue Louise and Boulevard de Waterloo area; inexpensive fashions are along Rue Neuve, Lower Town; and smart boutiques and antique shops in the Place du Grand Sablon. For genteel shopping head for the Galeries St Hubert. Bear in mind that if you want diamonds and cutting-edge fashion, take a morning out to vist Antwerp – the range is superior and prices more reasonable. Brussels' markets are the place for antiques (*see* page 21) while department stores are located throughout town. Shopping hours are 10:00–18:00 Mon–Sat, sometimes longer. Many stores (food, books, etc.) are also open for a few hours on Sundays.

Diamonds

Antwerp is considered the best place in the world for cut diamonds, so it is worth hopping on the train and buying there – it's just 50 minutes away. Head for Antwerp's diamond district: the streets around Vestingstraat, Rijstraat and Hoveniersstraat (map H–C2/3).

Chocolates

Belgian chocolates are at nearly every corner. There are so many shops and while the most popular are

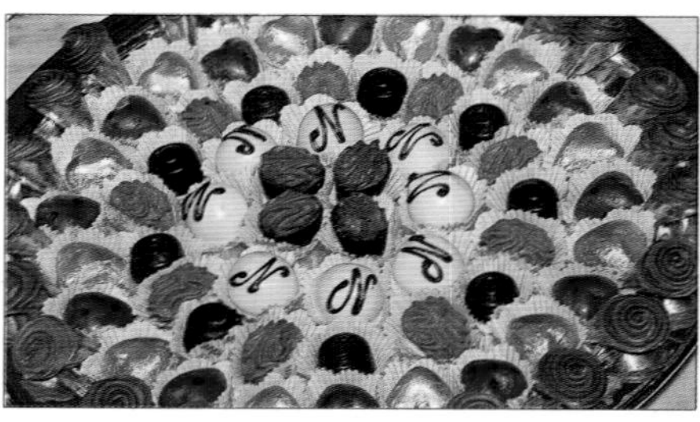

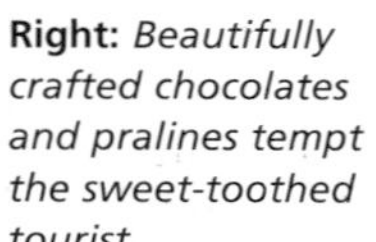

Right: *Beautifully crafted chocolates and pralines tempt the sweet-toothed tourist.*

good (many branches of **Godiva**, **Léonidas** and **Neuhaus**), some are divine.

Wittamer
This is where the rich and famous precipitate, for not only does the company fashion good chocolate *confiserie*, pralines and cakes, but it has an extraordinary imaginative flair too. You will even find Diana von Furstenberg in chocolate, right down to her bag and shoes. Possibly the best in Belgium?
✉ *place du Grand Sablon 6-12-13, B-1000,*
☎ *02 512 37 42 or 02 512 52 09,*
◷ *09:00–17:30 Mon–Sun.*

Pierre Marcolini
Sober décor and sombre packaging announce the luxuriously rich pralines created by this distinguished *chocolatier*.
✉ *place du Grand Sablon 39, B-1000,*
☎ *02 514 12 06, or*
✉ *avenue Louise 75M, B–1050,*
☎ *02 538 42 24.*

Food Stores

Au Suisse
A renowned deli and store selling delicious Belgian fare.
✉ *blvd Anspach 73, B-1000,*
☎ *02 512 95 89.*

Beer Mania
Offers a vast selection of beers.
✉ *Chaussée de Wavre, Ixelles, B-1050,*
☎ *02 512 17 88,*
💻 *www.beermania.be*

Dandoy
A selection of delicious biscuits and breads.
✉ *Rue au Beurre, B-1000,*
☎ *02 511 03 26.*

Books and Comics

Looking for an English-language book? Or Tintin's adventures?

Sterling Books
English-language books at sterling prices.
✉ *Rue du Fossé aux Loups, B-1000,*
☎ *02 223 62 23.*

Belgian Cheeses
Belgium produces some fine cheeses, though they are largely unknown outside the country. Look out for:
- **Rubens** – a semi-soft cow's-milk cheese with a brown rind (it was named for the painter).
- **Herve** – a brick-shaped, cow's-milk cheese that becomes spicy with age.
- **Bruxelles kaas** – a smooth, but strong and salty cheese made from cow's milk.

Best Buys
- **Belgian pralines** and **chocolates**.
- **Art books** and **posters** from the museum shops.
- **Belgian lace**, which is produced in many parts of the country.
- **Household goods**, with unusual design, packaging and gift items.
- **Contemporary fashion**.
- **Antiques** and bric-a-brac.
- **Diamonds** and **diamond jewellery**.
- **Belgian beer**.

Refreshing Moments

Le Pain Quotidien
Tearoom and snacks.
✉ rue A Dansaert 16, B-1000,
☎ 02 502 23 61;
✉ rue des Sablons 11, B-1000,
☎ 02 513 5154;
✉ ave Louise 124, B-1000,
☎ 02 646 49 83.

Le Cirio
An Art-Nouveau café-cum-bar.
✉ rue de la Bourse 18, B-1000,
☎ 02 512 13 95.

L'Atelier Gourmand
Highly-rated Uccle deli.
✉ rue Vandekindere 470, B-1050,
☎ 02 344 51 90.

Le Roi
Pricey café-bar.
✉ Grand-Place 1, B-1000,
☎ 02 513 08 70.

Waterstone's
Variety of English books.
✉ *blvd Adolphe Max 71–75, B-1000,*
☎ *02 219 27 08.*

La Boutique Tintin
Books, and more, on this famous character.
✉ *rue de la Colline 13, B-1000,*
☎ *02 514 51 52.*

Fnac
Good selection of French and English books, CDs, audio-visual gear, etc.
✉ *rue Neuve, City 2, B-1000,*
☎ *02 275 11 11.*

Fashion
Antwerp is *the* place but Rue Antoine Dansaert is the centre for Brussels' fashion.

Annemie Verbeke
Separates and dresses for women.
✉ *rue Antoine Dansaert 64,*
☎ *02 511 21 71.*

Azniv Afsar
Innovative mixes in women's fashion.
✉ *rue Léon Lepage 28, B-1000,*
☎ *02 512 30 96.*

Kaat Tilley
Separates, dresses and wedding dresses.
✉ *galerie du Roi 4, B-1000,*
☎ *02 514 07 63.*

Nicolas Woit
Asian-inspired fabrics and women's clothing.
✉ *rue Antoine Dansaert 80, B-1000,*
☎ *02 503 48 32.*

Household Goods
The area around Rue Blaes and Rue Haute (great for furnishings and the weekly market – *see* page 21) is a good hunting ground for household items.

Au Tapis Magique
Good carpets for bargain hunters.
✉ *place du Jeu de Balle 7, B-1000,*
☎ *02 511 01 63.*

Les 2 Extrêmes
From smart to cute, and china to decorative items, this store lives up to its name.

✉ *rue du Lombard 33, B-1000,*
☎ *02 502 03 06.*

La Vaisselle au Kilo
Not everything is sold by the kilo, but there are lots of good pottery and ceramic ideas at excellent prices.
✉ *rue Bodenbroek 8a, B-1000,*
☎ *02 513 49 84.*

New De Wolf
Household and decorative ideas.
✉ *rue Haute 91, B-1000,*
☎ *02 511 10 18.*

Department Stores

They don't have the popularity of British stores, but still represent good if traditional value for money.

INNO
Large department store, with two central branches.
✉ *rue Neuve 111, B-1000,*
☎ *02 211 21 11;*
✉ *avenue Louise 12, B-1050.*

Above: *Lace is one of the country's best-known crafts.*
Opposite: *The best fashion is show-cased in Antwerp.*

Lace

From Antwerp to Ghent, Bruges to Brussels, handmade (and machine-made) Belgian lace is a great buy.

Manufacture Belge des Dentelles
Exquisite lace gifts and trimmings.
✉ *galerie de la Reine 6–8, B-1000,*
☎ *02 511 44 77.*

Gobelins Art
Lace items, trimmings, tapestries and gifts.
✉ *rue Charles Buls 6–10, B-1000,*
☎ *02 512 09 41.*

Markets

One of Brussels' great attractions. *See* Highlights, page 21.

Tax-free Shopping
Visitors to Brussels who do not hold EU passports can reclaim their Sales Tax (TVA in Belgium) when they leave the country.
The goods themselves, accompanied by their receipts, must be shown to the customs department at the airport along with a sales tax claim form which the customs has duly stamped. This can then be mailed back to the address provided and most, if not all, of the sales tax will be refunded.

Above: *Today's smart Hotel Amigo was once an infamous prison.*

Stars and Prices
Hotels in Belgium are graded on the star system though they are usually awarded stars on the quantity (rather than quality) of their facilities.

Note that prices for accommodation drop quite considerably over weekends (the bureaucrats go home) and during the politically quiet season – July and August. It is quite acceptable to ask a hotel for a discount at these times.

WHERE TO STAY

For a city of around one million inhabitants, Brussels has plenty of accommodation – thanks to the needs of the burgeoning European community. However, these foreign residents are also the cause of the city's high hotel prices.

It makes sense to choose a hotel that either suits your needs or your pocket. But be warned: business travellers are usually uninterested in charm and look for hotels that are clean, functional and with good business facilities, so don't expect a vast choice loaded with character and creativity.

If the purpose of a visit is to enjoy the architecture, museums and artistic sights, then the **historic centre** puts you into the heart of town. Much is either within walking distance or accessible by bus, métro or taxi.

If time is of no great concern, try the **suburbs** where hotels are located in greener residential areas, with village-like communities. Uccle and Ixelles are both good options.

Eurocrats with business in the **European section** of Brussels will want locally based accommodation. Many hotels and apartments are to be found near **Rue de la Loi**, while beyond **La Cinquantenaire** lies a neighbourhood that borders on the large park. This area offers a number of hotels with quite a different feel to them and the village-like atmosphere is very attractive.

Belgium is geographically small and although most sights can be reached from the capital, the historic and artistic towns of **Bruges**, **Antwerp** and **Ghent** merit a longer stay. For those who want to stay overnight here, we have included a short list of recommendations for these three centres.

Historic Centre

• Luxury

Hotel Amigo (Map C–C4)
From an old prison to a large, modern hotel, this luxury hostelry stands out with its clean lines, modern décor and excellent service. Northern rooms face the tower of the Town Hall. A well-priced restaurant with traditional and international cuisine. A good central position behind the Town Hall. Parking in garage.
✉ *rue de l'Amigo 1–3, B-1000, Brussels,* ☎ *02 547 47 47,* ℻ *02 513 52 77,* 💻 *www.rfhotels.com* 🖱 *hotelamigo@hotelamigo.com*

Carrefour de L'Europe (Map C–D4)
This central, mid-sized hotel overlooks the Marché aux Herbes. The sights of central Brussels are all within walking distance. Parking.
✉ *rue Marché aux Herbes 110, B-1000,* ☎ *02 504 94 00,* ℻ *02 504 95 00,* 🖱 *info@carrefoureurope.net*

Radisson SAS Hotel (Map C–D3)
One of Brussels' more modern hotels (just over 10 years old), despite its Art-Deco façade. Rooms range from modern to traditional. Conveniently located behind the Marché aux Herbes.
✉ *rue du Fossé aux Loups 47, B-1000,* ☎ *02 219 28 28,* ℻ *02 219 62 62,* 💻 *www.radissonsas.com* 🖱 *info@radissonsas.com*

Le Dixseptième (Map C–D4)
This hotel is small, elegant and breathes character. A beautifully converted period building, now hosts a fine, quiet hotel. Lovely rooms, very central.
✉ *rue de la Madeleine 25, B-1000, Brussels,* ☎ *02 502 57 44,* ℻ *02 502 64 24,* 💻 *www.ledixseptieme.com* 🖱 *info@ledixseptieme.com*

Métropole (Map C–D2)
Judicious renovations have restored this old hotel to the grandeur of its 1895 opening year. Art-Deco, Art-Nouveau and even mock-Renaissance interior design dazzle the gaze in the public rooms. Parking.
✉ *place de Brouckère 31,* ☎ *02 217 23 00,* ℻ *02 218 02 20,* 💻 *www.metropolehotel.com* 🖱 *info@metropolehotel.be*

• Mid-range

Ibis Off Grand-Place (Map C–D4)
A large hotel in fine brick, very well placed behind the Grand-Place and within walking distance of many sights. Parking.
✉ *rue Marché aux Herbes 100, B-1000,* ☎ *02 514 40 40,* ℻ *02 514 50 67,* 💻 *www.ibishotel.com* 🖱 *H1046-RE@accor-hotels.com*

Alfa Sablon
(Map C–D5)
Close to the Place du Grand Sablon, this quiet, mid-sized hotel has largish rooms with good facilities. Smarter duplex suites are also available. Central sights are within walking distance. Parking nearby.
✉ *rue de la Paille 2–4, B-1000, Brussels,*
☎ *02 513 60 40,*
📠 *02 511 81 41,*
💻 *www.nh-hotels.com*
🖱 *info@alfasablon.gth.be*

Citadines Sainte Catherine
(Map C–C2)
In a culinarily active part of town (restaurants abound and the local market is excellent), an apartment-style hotel offering bright studio rooms with kitchenettes. It's just a 10-minute walk to Grand-Place.
✉ *quai au Bois à Bruler 51, B-1000 Brussels,*
☎ *02 221 14 113,*
📠 *02 221 14 11,*
💻 *www.citadines.com*
🖱 *stecatherine@citadines.com*

Atlas Hotel Brussels
(Map C–B3)
A well-priced, mid-sized, central hotel with comfortable rooms. Also rooms with kitchenettes. Parking nearby.
✉ *rue du Vieux Marché aux Grains 30, B-1000, Brussels,*
☎ *02 502 60 06,*
📠 *02 502 69 35,*
💻 *www.atlas.be*
🖱 *info@atlas.be*

La Madeleine
(Map C–D4)
Mid-sized hotel with pleasant rooms; quietest at the back. Plenty of restaurants and shops. A five-minute walk to Grand-Place. Parking nearby.
✉ *rue de la Montagne 20–22, B-1000, Brussels,*
☎ *02 513 29 73,*
📠 *02 502 13 50,*
💻 *www.hotel-la-madeleine.be*
🖱 *hotel-la-madeleine@hotel-la-madeleine.be*

Comfort Art Hotel Siru (Map C–E1)
At the top end of Rue Neuve, an unexciting Art-Deco exterior in a slightly run-down area belies the extraordinary interior. The functional rooms are decorated with original works by Belgian artists. Quieter rooms at the back. Hotel parking.
✉ *place Charles Rogier 1,*
☎ *02 203 35 80,*
📠 *02 203 33 03,*
💻 *www.comforthotel.siru.com*
🖱 *art.hotel.siru@skynet.be*

• ***BUDGET***

George V (Map C–A4)
Not as luxurious as its Parisian namesake, this hotel in the Ste Catherine area is however very central and ideal for families. Parking is available.
✉ *rue T'Kint 23, B-1000, Brussels,*
☎ *02 513 50 93,*
📠 *02 513 44 93,*
💻 *www.george5.com*
🖱 *reservations@george5.com*

Mozart (Map C–D4)
A well-priced, smart little hotel behind the

Grand-Place. Previously owned by Moroccans, it has a delightfully exotic atmosphere. Rooms only have showers. Ask for a rear room if you want tranquillity.

✉ *rue du Marché aux Fromages 23, B-1000,*
☎ *02 502 66 61,*
📠 *02 502 77 58,*
💻 *www.hotel-mozart.be*
🖱 *hotel.mozart@skynet.be*

Aux Arcades
(Map C–D3)
On the Rue des Bouchers (*the* street for seafood), this small, simple but comfortable hotel is in the heart of historic Brussels. In a pedestrian-only street, though paying parking is nearby.

✉ *rue des Bouchers 36, B-1000, Brussels,*
☎ *02 511 28 76,*
📠 *02 511 26 52.*

Hotel Welcome
(Map C–C2)
A real find: charming owners, innovative attitudes and superb value for money. Individually styled rooms. Well-placed for the centre; next to La Truite d'Argent restaurant (*see* page 66). Ten rooms. Parking.

✉ *rue du Peuplier 5, B-1000 Brussels,*
☎ *02 219 95 46,*
📠 *02 217 18 87,*
💻 *www.hotelwelcome.com*
🖱 *info@hotelwelcome.com*

Hotel Noga
(Map C–B2)
A cosy, small hotel with unique charm. Unusual decoration and pleasant owners. Nearby parking and historic centre within walking distance.

✉ *rue du Béguinage 38, B-1000, Brussels,*
☎ *02 218 67 63,*
📠 *02 218 16 03,*
💻 *www.nogahotel.com*
🖱 *info@nogahotel.com*

European Quarter

• *Luxury*

Dorint Hotel Brussels
(Map E–E4)
In the heart of European Brussels, minutes' walk from many international companies, this state-of-the-art hotel with its chic dark stone, chrome and glass interior is both welcoming and professional. A fine restaurant and paying parking garage (street parking is also available).

✉ *boulevard Charlemagne 11–19, B-1000, Brussels,*
☎ *02 231 09 09,*
📠 *02 230 33 71,*
💻 *www.dorint.com*
🖱 *info.brubru@dorint.com*

• *Mid-range*

Park Hotel
(Map E–H5)
On the tree-lined avenue behind the Cinquantenaire monument, this comfortable hotel, created from some elegant patrician townhouses, has a cosy but efficient ambience. Near the European business district, and yet just minutes from the Ring. No restaurant but good buffet breakfast. Garage and street parking.

avenue de l'Yser 21, B-1040, Brussels,
☎ *02 735 74 00,*
02 735 19 67,
www.parkhotelbrussels.be
info@parkhotelbrussels.be

Hotel Leopold
(Map E–B5)
Traditional hotel in a good location close to European Parliament and the Place du Luxembourg. Parking.
rue du Luxembourg 35, B-1050,
☎ *02 511 18 28,*
02 514 19 39,
www.hotel-leopold.be
reservations@hotel-leopold.be

• ***BUDGET***

Lambeau (Map E–I4)
Family-run hotel in a quiet residential neighbourhood. City centre is easily accessible by public transport. Parking.
avenue Lambeau 150, B-1200, Brussels,
☎ *02 732 51 70,*
02 732 54 90,
www.hotellambeau.com
info@hotellambeau.com

Les Bluets
(Map D–A2)
It's worth the ride to this quirky little hotel near the Boulevard de Waterloo / Avenue de la Toison d'Or. This family-run, non-smoking hotel oozes character, with its myriad plants and unusual bric-a-brac.
rue Berckmans 124, B-1060, Brussels,
☎ *02 534 39 83,*
02 543 09 70,
www.geocities.com/les_bluets
bluets@swing.be

Further Afield

• ***LUXURY***

Conrad International Brussels (Map D–B1)
A grand hotel in Ixelles' swankiest shopping street. Luxurious and glitzy, the furnishings ooze expense. Magnificent stained glass in its pricey brasserie. Private paying parking.
avenue Louise 71, B-1050, Brussels,
☎ *02 542 42 42,*
02 542 42 00,
www.brussels.conradinternational.com
brusselsinfo@conradhotels.com

• ***MID-RANGE***

Agenda Louise
(Map D–B2)
Amid shops and restaurants, a good, quiet address. Parking.
rue de Florence 6–8, B-1000, Belgium,
☎ *02 539 00 31,*
02 539 00 63,
www.hotel-agenda.com
louise@hotel-agenda.com

Les Tourelles
(Map D–B6)
A bus or tram ride from the centre to Uccle, this comfortable hotel is a great alternative to the more expensive central ones.
avenue Winston Churchill 135, B-1180,
☎ *02 344 02 84,*
02 346 42 70,
www.lestourelles.be
info@lestourelles.be

Out of Town

• *LUXURY*

T'Sandt (Antwerp) (Map H–A2)
Tucked away in a side street, this renovated neo-Rococo building has masses of character and is very central to the historic heart of Antwerp. Private and street parking.
✉ *Het Zand 17–19, 2000 Antwerp,*
☎ *03 232 93 90,*
📠 *03 232 56 13,*
💻 *www.hotel-sandt.be*
🖱 *info@hotel-sandt.be*

Romantik Pand Hotel (Bruges) (Map F–B2)
Attractive, renovated townhouses just off Bruges' picturesque Dijver, this centrally located, elegant hotel has a great charm. Superb breakfasts.
✉ *Pandreitje 16, 8000 Bruges,*
☎ *050 34 06 66,*
📠 *050 34 05 56,*
💻 *www.pandhotel.com*
🖱 *info@pandhotel.com*

Sofitel Gent Belfort (Ghent) (Map G–B1)
A good hotel with full facilities in a pleasant building in the heart of the city. Good restaurant. Parking.
✉ *Hoogpoort 63, 9000 Ghent,*
☎ *09 233 33 31,*
📠 *09 233 11 02,*
💻 *www.sofitel.com*
🖱 *HI673-HR@accor.hotels.be*

• *MID-RANGE*

Gravensteen (Ghent) (Map G–B1)
In a fine but slightly tired period building. A quirky but friendly hotel between luxury and mid-range. Ideally placed for the historic centre. Private parking.
✉ *Jan Breyelstraat 35, 9000 Ghent,*
☎ *09 225 11 50,*
📠 *09 225 18 50,*
💻 *www.gravensteen.be*
🖱 *hotel@gravensteen.be*

• *BUDGET*

Rubenshof (Antwerp) (Map H–A4)
Good location for a small family-run hotel. Located in a former cardinal's mansion.
✉ *Amerikalei 115–117, 2000 Antwerp,*
☎ *03 237 07 89,*
📠 *03 248 25 94,*
🖱 *rubenshf@xs4all.be*

Anselmus (Bruges) (Map F–C1)
An attractive, friendly, clean and well-placed hotel at the upper end of budget. Excellent breakfasts included. Parking nearby.
✉ *Ridderstraat 15, 8000 Bruges,*
☎ *050 34 13 74,*
📠 *050 34 19 16,*
💻 *www.anselmus.be*
🖱 *info@anselmus.be*

Hotel Erasmus (Ghent) (Map G–A1)
A delightful family-run hotel in a traditional old building just steps away from the Korenlei and canal. Quiet garden. Parking nearby.
✉ *Poel 25, 9000 Ghent,*
☎ *09 224 21 95,*
📠 *09 233 42 41,*
💻 *www.proximedia.com/web/hotel-erasmus.html*

Culinary Kudos

Ettekeis • spicy meat balls
Friture • a take-away box of French fries (chips)
Gueuze • Belgian beer type made from different brews, all refermented in the bottle
Kip-kap • a pressed meat dish made with offal and other animal pieces
Kriek • beer flavoured with cherry
Lambic • naturally fermented beer
Pain à la Greque • sweet biscuits with caramelized sugar
Praline • a single, pre-moulded Belgian chocolate
Ribbeke • pork ribs
Stoemp • a potato and vegetable purée
Waterzooi • a casserole of fish or chicken and vegetables
Witlof • Belgian endive (chicory)

EATING OUT
What to Eat

The French may consider their cuisine the finest in the world, but many of their Belgian neighbours question their supremacy. And, with Brussels taking an increasingly important role in European politics, restaurants are catering for a growing international and more discerning clientele. This means that local Franco-Belgian restaurants now compete with a wide range of foreign restaurants, in particular Italian, Asian and Middle Eastern.

Belgians are hearty eaters and love their meals. They snack frequently (and with all those chocolate shops, potato chip sellers and *sandwicheries*, temptation is on every street) and dine well. They also drink copiously, but that is discussed elsewhere.

With a change in taste and the influx of foreigners in town, Belgian eating habits have matured during the last three decades. Portions have become smaller, though they remain more generous than those offered by the French, and a whole etiquette has developed around *La Cuisine Belge* with the result that there are some remarkable young chefs dedicated to satsifying the most discerning of tastes. And, as the capital, Brussels has the pick of the crop (distances are short between mountain and sea, so produce is very fresh) and will feature dishes from all parts of the country.

Below: *Belgium produces some excellent cheeses.*

Soups and starters are usually copious and warming in winter. Vegetables, *bouillons*, cereals and game might flavour a *soupe* or *potage*, while cold cuts will comprise

slices of pork, beef and fowl, including offal and parts of the head.

Those home-cooked favourites number dishes such as ***lapin au lambic***, an aromatic preparation of rabbit stewed in beer; ***lapin aux pruneaux***, rabbit stewed with prunes;

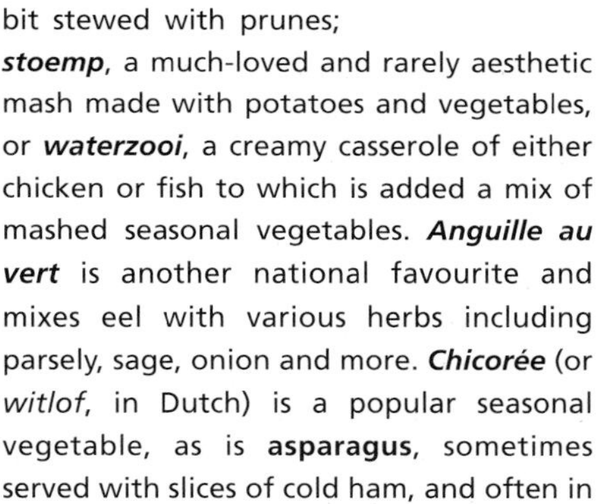

stoemp, a much-loved and rarely aesthetic mash made with potatoes and vegetables, or ***waterzooi***, a creamy casserole of either chicken or fish to which is added a mix of mashed seasonal vegetables. ***Anguille au vert*** is another national favourite and mixes eel with various herbs including parsely, sage, onion and more. ***Chicorée*** (or *witlof*, in Dutch) is a popular seasonal vegetable, as is **asparagus**, sometimes served with slices of cold ham, and often in a creamy béchamel sauce.

In winter, **game** is to be found on most menus. *Chevreuil* (venison), *faison* (pheasant), *lièvre* (hare); and *canard*, (duck), are all carefully prepared – usually with sauces and seasonal vegetables and, inevitably, with French fries. Naturally, steak, lamb, pork and veal are year-round regulars on the menu.

On the seafood front, there are superb displays of fresh **shellfish**: North Sea **fish** and **crustaceans** are among the more pricey dishes. But, of course, there are still those ***moules***. It is rare, these days, to find exquisite mussels as too many inexpensive restaurants cash in on the tradition. However, among our listings there are some reputable establishments which serve mussels

Above: *Seafood is one of Brussels' best bets.*

Coffee
In Brussels a good, strong espresso-style *café* (served with an individually wrapped chocolate) is normally drunk as a quick caffeine intake, but plenty of locals devote time to sitting down over a *café au lait* or a *café creme* and one of those delightful pastries. *Café American* is either instant coffee or a very weak filter coffee – if that's your brew, make a point of asking for it.

Chips and *Frites*
Traditionally Belgium has been known for its *moules-frites*, mussels from the North Sea and French fries. These are usually served with lashings of mayonnaise, and a variety of mayonnaise-based sauces.

Beer
There are three main types of beer, differentiated by the type of fermentation:

Pilsen or **blond beer** fermented at a low temperature. Breweries to look out for include Alken-Maes and Interbrew; and the spicier Münchener, Wiener or Dortmunder.

Special beers which are brewed at higher temperatures (15–20°C), such as those produced by the Trappists in Cistercian abbeys. Look out for beers from Chimay or Rochefort.

Lambic, **krieks** and **gueuzes** are the result of spontaneous fermentation without additives to encourage the process. They are then left to mature in kegs and finally bottled. The **lambic** ferments a second time in its bottle and changes its name to **gueuze**. The **Krieks** are red in colour, often the result of adding fruit, such as cherries, to their fermentation vats. For a young lambic (called a **faro**) look out for **Cantillon Faro** and **Drie Fonteinen**, who also make a good gueuze.

Belgium is the only country which ages ales. Have a look for the old brown such as **Oud Bruin Ongefilterd**.

au naturel; with tomato sauce; *moules marinières* (with white wine and cream); with beer sauces and even with pasta.

Belgians have a collective sweet tooth. Many patisseries and *chocolateries* testify to their prowess in the field of **cakes**, **chocolates** and feather-light **pastries**. Tarts, caramelized and stewed fruits served in delicate biscuit baskets, spicy and crumbling biscuits, and gateaux are all much appreciated.

And don't forget Belgian **cheeses** (*see* panel, page 51, for suggestions). You probably won't be familiar with their names but Belgium does produce some excellent hard and soft cheeses. Ask to see the cheese trolley in the better restaurants and try some of their own, home-grown cheeses such as the *potkès*, salted fresh white cheese, or Rubens.

What to Drink

Belgium does not produce (in any quantity) wines of its own. Thus wine-lovers will have to buy or order imported wines. French wines are ubiqitous but diners will also have a choice of Italian, Spanish, German, Australian, South African and Californian wines. The country is also known for its bottled water: Spa is the most famous and a good sparkling or non-fizzy water. However, it is for its beer that Belgium is justly famous (*see* panel). Some diners will accompany their meal with beer, others will snack while drinking beer at a bar or café. And, unlike in many other countries, the beers will be served in a range of attractive glasses, usually a round cup or a glass, produced by the beer manufacturers.

Where to Eat

Tourists inevitably head for the **Grand-Place**. It is both a good idea as well as an error: the prices are high, geared for tourists; menus are not always creative, and restaurants are invariably crowded. On the plus side the buildings provide a magnificent backdrop. But push on round that corner and find some of the less obvious restaurants – they serve the less obvious dishes too.

For more upmarket dining, the area around **Place du Grand Sablon** is chic and easily accessible, though often pricey. **Ste Catherine** has developed a firm following among locals for the variety of fish-inspired menus and competitively priced restaurants. Again, this area is easily accessible by foot (or métro). The **EU area** has some good Italian and Spanish restaurants (cheap, cheerful and spilling out onto the pavement in summer), while the more adventurous tourist will take to **Ixelles** where the numerous Belgian bistros are in competition with newer imported cuisines. Good Indian and Bengali food abounds.

If you haven't a clue what to eat and wish to be inspired, stroll northwards from the Grand-Place, cross the Marché aux Herbes and continue via Rue des Bouchers or Rue du Marché aux Peaux into Rue des Bouchers. Along the way, the fragrance of far shores will tempt you: Arab, Chinese, Greek, Italian, Japanese, Spanish and Turkish restaurants all vie for business.

Asparagus Mania
April to June is asparagus season and the Belgians feast on these delicious veggies as though there were no tomorrow. Eat them Flemish-style with finely-chopped boiled eggs, melted butter and parsley; in a light soufflé, or salad-style, cold with a vinaigrette. Even a Hollandaise sauce helps them slip down easily. Etiquette dictates... what? Nowadays, asparagus lovers eat the whole stem, starting from the tip, and it is considered just as appropriate to eat with the hands as with a fork.

Below: *Wines and spirits take a back seat in pubs and cafés: beer is the most popular beverage.*

Historic Centre

• LUXURY

Comme Chez Soi
Still considered by many, though debated by some, as Brussels' finest restaurant. Pierre Wynants merits all the accolades and getting a table requires advance planning – up to a month or more. However, armed with a credit card and good company, it is definitely worth the wait.
⊠ *place Rouppe 23, B-1000, Brussels,*
☎ *02 512 29 21.*

Villa Lorraine
Elegant without being too sober, a garden backdrop for one of the city's smartest addresses. A smart chef's shop offers the less well-heeled some affordable culinary delights. Reservations.
⊠ *avenue du Vivier d'Oie 75, B-1000, Brussels,*
☎ *02 374 31 63.*

La Maison du Cygne
Old-world decor, plenty of wood and white linen, and right on the Grand-Place. Serves traditional Belgian dishes.
⊠ *rue Charles Buyl 2, B-1000, Brussels,*
☎ *02 511 82 44.*

Aux Armes de Bruxelles
Traditional restaurant with a Franco-Belgian menu. Specialities include seafood.
⊠ *rue des Bouchers 13, B-1000, Brussels,*
☎ *02 511 55 50,*
💻 *www.armebrux.be*

Samourai
Japanese at its pricey best. A full range of national specialities including sushi, sashimi and tempura. Attractive and simple decor.
⊠ *rue du Fossé aux Loups 28, B-1000,*
☎ *02 217 56 39.*

La Belle Maraîcheire
Another popular and highly recommended seafood restaurant. A rather ordinary interior but top-class French cuisine.
⊠ *place Sainte Catherine 11, B-1000,*
☎ *02 512 97 59.*

• MID-RANGE

Armand & Ko
A smart, trendy restaurant that serves good, traditional dishes. Emphasis on presentation and fresh ingredients.
⊠ *rue des Chapeliers 16, B-1000, Brussels,*
☎ *02 514 17 63,*
💻 *www. armandandko.be*

Les Petits Oignons
In the heart of Sablon, this cosy restaurant features first-class French cuisine. Interesting interior.
⊠ *rue Notre Seigneur 13, B-1000, Brussels,*
☎ *02 512 47 38,*
💻 *www. petits-oignons.be*

Bonsoir Clara
In the trendy neighbourhood around Place Saint Géry, a modern restaurant, interesting ambience

with cast-iron and brick decor, subtle lighting over stainless steel tables. Franco-Belgian cuisine.

✉ *rue Antoine Dansaert 22, B-1000,*
☎ *02 502 09 90.*

Chez Léon

Well known, always full and very touristy, but still serves good *moules-frites*. Apart from the ever-popular mussels, this bustling restaurant with fairly bright, ordinary decor, does other fishy things very well and asks fair prices.

✉ *rue des Bouchers 18, B-1000, Brussels,*
☎ *02 511 14 15.*

Scheltema

Clean, modern interior for this good restaurant specializing in seafood.

✉ *rue des Dominicains 7, B-1000, Brussels,*
☎ *02 512 20 84.*

L'Estrille du Vieux Bruxelles

In a row where dozens of small restaurants spill out onto the street, a stone's throw from Grand Sablon, this restaurant is in a 16th-century building. Elegant and specializing in classical Belgian cuisine.

✉ *rue de Rollebeek 7, B-1000, Brussels,*
☎ *02 512 58 57.*

L'Ombrello

Modern, no-frills decor for this Tuscan restaurant. In summer it overflows onto the attractive square. Good pastas and fish dishes.

✉ *place Sainte Catherine 4, B-1000, Brussels,*
☎ *02 513 68 34.*

Le Grand Mayeur

Gypsies meet Belgians in this well-known Brussels rendezvous, a restaurant full of

Above: *Pedestrian-only streets and squares encourage pavement service at restaurants and cafés.*

Seafood Unravelled

Gourmet seafood menus will often offer a bewildering array of shellfish. Here are some to look out for:

Buccins • whelks
Coques • cockles
Couteau • razor shells
Crabe • crab
Crevettes • shrimps
Crevettes roses • prawns
Écrevisse • fresh-water crayfish
Gambas • large prawns
Homard • lobster
Huitres • oysters
Langouste • prawns or scampi
Langouste • crayfish
Moules • mussels
Palourdes • clams
Tourteau • a type of crab

character. Ambience probably better than the cuisine but with live music in evenings, worth the visit. Book for week-end dinners.

✉ *place du Grand Sablon 43, B-1000, Brussels,*
☎ *02 512 80 91.*

La Truite d'Argent
An excellent seafood restaurant, on the site of the historic fish market (now a tree-lined square with a pool). Traditional interior and good menu. This is a very popular place for fish menus and if this restaurant is full, try another in the area.

✉ *quai au Bois à Bruler 23, B-1000, Brussels,*
☎ *02 219 95 46.*

Lola
In the fashionable part of the city centre, a popular contemporary restaurant with inventive French cuisine. Full on Grand Sablon market days. Bookings advisable.

✉ *place du Grand Sablon 33, B-1000, Brussels,*
☎ *02 514 24 60.*

Le Vieux Bruxelles
A spectacular display of seafood lures one inside to an airy, modern environment, slightly different from others in the street.

✉ *rue des Bouchers 33–35, B-1000, Brussels,*
☎ *02 511 24 57.*

Au Vieux St Martin
A favourite hangout for those doing the markets at the week-end. Good food (from snacks to more extensive dishes), modern decor, and very popular with locals.

✉ *place du Grand Sablon 38, B-1000, Brussels,*
☎ *02 512 64 76.*

• ***BUDGET***

L'Achepot
A small, cosy, family-run *estaminet* tavern-cum-restaurant with traditional Belgian home cooking at very affordable prices.

✉ *place Sainte Catherine 1, B-1000, Brussels,*
☎ *02 511 62 21.*

't Kelderke
Open daily, a cosy cellar restaurant with consistently good typical Belgian cuisine. Frequented as much by locals as by tourists.

✉ *Grand-Place 15, B-1000, Brussels,*
☎ *02 513 73 44.*

Les Larmes du Tigre
Mouthwatering, and authentic Thai cuisine for connoisseurs.

✉ *rue Wynants 21, B-1000, Brussels,*
☎ *02 512 18 77.*

Kasbah
A delightfully pleasant yet smart address for Moroccan specialities. Reservations are advised.

✉ *rue Antoine Dansaert 20, B-1000, Brussels,*
☎ *02 520 40 26.*

La Cave de Yasmina
A simple Tunisian

restaurant with quick and delicious dishes.
✉ *rue Marché aux Fromages 9, B-1000, Brussels,*
☎ *02 512 83 40.*

Café Mokafe
Tuck into coffee and a slice of home-made cake at this people-watching place under the arcades.
✉ *Gallerie du Roi 9, B-1000, Brussels,*
☎ *02 511 78 70.*

Dandoy
Brussels specialities and biscuits in this shop that has become an institution.
✉ *rue au Beurre 31, B-1000, Brussels,*
☎ *02 511 03 26;*
✉ *rue Charles Buls 14, B-1000, Brussels,*
☎ *02 512 65 88.*

Bombay Inn
Not very promising from the outside, but offers a warm welcome and a good menu at affordable prices.
✉ *rue de la Fourche 38, B-1000, Brussels,*
☎ *02 219 59 54.*

Corné Toison d'Or
A fabulous address for delicious chocolates in very beautiful wrapping.
✉ *galerie du Roi 24–26, B-1000, Brussels,*
☎ *02 512 49 84.*

Further Afield

• *LUXURY*

L'Atelier de la Truffe Noire
Specializing in Italian cuisine, truffles abound at this fashionable and contemporarily styled eatery. Its sister restaurant, an even smarter Italian restaurant, also featuring truffles, is out towards Cambre. Also highly recommended.
✉ *ave Louise 300, B-1050, Brussels,*
☎ *02 640 54 55,*
💻 *www.truffenoire.com*

La Truffe Noire
✉ *boulevard de la Cambre 12, B-1050, Brussels,*
☎ *02 640 44 22,*
💻 *www.truffenoire.com*

• *MID-RANGE*

La Quincaillerie Brasserie
A converted hardware store is an unusual and stylish venue for one of the city's most popular restaurants. Largely Franco-Belgian, it is also known for its seafood.
✉ *rue du Page 45, B-1050, Brussels,*
☎ *02 533 98 33.*

Le Living Room
Very popular for its eclectic mix of Asian cuisine in an equally unusually decorated interior.
✉ *chaussée de Charleroi 50, B-1060, Brussels,*
☎ *02 534 44 34.*

Le Temps Delire
Near Avenue Louise and the Musée Horta, this interesting restaurant has a typical French menu but is set in a stripped-down and trendily decorated Belgian building.
✉ *chaussée de Charleroi 175–177, B-1060, Brussels,*
☎ *02 538 12 10.*

Le Cosmopolite

A popular brasserie in the EU part of town, with good lunches as well as dinners.

✉ *ave de Cortenberg 36, B-1040, Brussels,*
☎ *02 280 18 70.*

Au Palais des Indes

Smart Indian restaurant, not the curry-house variety. Crisp napkins and ties abound. Excellent traditional Indian dishes with tandoor favourites.

✉ *avenue Louise 263, B-1050, Brussels,*
☎ *02 646 09 41.*

Amadeus

Once Rodin's studio, now a trendy and romantic venue for great Franco-Belgian cuisine.

✉ *rue Veydt 13, B-1050, Brussels,*
☎ *02 538 34 27.*

• *BUDGET*

Volle Gas

A traditional Belgian brasserie in the centre of Ixelles, decorated with marble and cast-iron tables, posters and bottles of wine. Terrace seating and live jazz music in summertime. Very popular with locals.

✉ *place Fernand Cocq 21, B-1050, Brussels,*
☎ *02 502 89 17.*

Le Grain de Sel

Better food than one might imagine from this small restaurant in Ixelles. An imaginative menu and good prices.

✉ *Chaussée de Vleurgat, B-1050, Brussels,*
☎ *02 648 18 58.*

La Grande Porte

Just by the Polish church, a typical Brussels estaminet bistro-cum-bar with all the favourite local dishes, perennially popular. Dark and smoky, loaded with atmosphere.

✉ *rue Notre Seigneur 9, B-1000, Brussels,*
☎ *02 512 89 98.*

Le Gout des Autres

Near the Place aux Balle flea market, a small North African menu, in a delightful Moroccan setting. Convivial (warm-yellow) ambience and excellent food. A good bet for Saturday or Sunday lunch.

✉ *rue Haute 189, B-1000, Brussels,*
☎ *02 502 02 38.*

Bazaar

Trendy interior, a menu that moves from west to east, and a comfortable ambience with interesting decor.

✉ *rue des Capucins 63, B-1000, Brussels,*
☎ *02 511 20 00.*

Le Pré aux Clercs

Just beyond the Museum de l'Armée, and at the less expensive end of moderate, this small Italian restaurant is directed with a flourish by its chef/owner. Good Italian dishes (including home-made pasta) with some Belgian concessions.

✉ *ave de la Renaissance 42,*

B-1040, Brussels,
☎ *02 735 15 08.*

Dolma
Vegetarian by definition but enjoyed by the odd carnivore too, this restaurant with shop is popular and has a light, creative menu.
✉ *chaussée d'Ixelles 329, B-1050, Brussels,*
☎ *02 649 89 81.*

Le Hasard des Choses
Unassuming, low-key but very highly rated neighbourhood restaurant. Belgian and French dishes.
✉ *rue du Page 31, B-1050, Brussels,*
☎ *02 538 18 63.*

Out of Town

• *LUXURY*

De Matelote (Antwerp)
Possibly Antwerp's finest fish restaurant, tucked away in a narrow street just two blocks from the Scheldt. Intimate atmosphere and the freshest of seafoods.
✉ *Haarstraat 9, B-2000 Antwerp,*
☎ *03 231 32 07.*

De Snippe (Bruges)
A renowned restaurant with not only good cuisine but a wonderfully romantic ambience. Located in the canal-side hotel of the same name.
✉ *Nieuwe Gentweg 53, B-8000, Bruges,*
☎ *050 33 70 70,*
💻 *www.desnippe.be*

• *MID-RANGE*

Bhavani (Bruges)
It may seem strange to eat Indian cuisine in Bruges, but people come for miles to eat at Bhavani. Outstanding cuisine based on recipes from many regions of India.
✉ *Simon Stevin plein 5, B-8000, Bruges,*
☎ *050 33 90 25,*
💻 *www.bhavani.be*

Den Dyver (Bruges)
A pleasant restaurant in an old Flemish building right on the canal. Imaginative cuisine with the accent on incorporating beer in its dishes.
✉ *Dijver 5, B–8000, Bruges,*
☎ *050 33 60 69.*

• *BUDGET*

't Zolderke (Antwerp)
An interesting interior, dining on three floors in a 16th-century house. Good atmosphere, friendly place serving Belgian food. Near the cathedral.
✉ *Hoofdkerkstraat 7, B-2000, Antwerp,*
☎ *03 233 84 27.*

Het Vermoeide Model (Antwerp)
Immensely popular, simple and inexpensive, serving good Belgian fare. Reservations advised.
✉ *Lijnwaadmarkt 2, B-2000, Antwerp,*
☎ *03 233 52 61.*

Rock Fort (Bruges)
Fine innovative cuisine from a couple of young restaurateurs in search of authentic European flavours. Simple decor.
✉ *Langestraat 15, B-8000, Bruges,*
☎ *050 33 41 13.*

Clubs, Pubs and Bars
À la Mort Subite, ✉ rue des Montagnes aux Herbes Potagères 7, ☎ 02 513 13 18.
L'Amour Fou, ✉ chaussée d'Ixelles 185, Place Fernand Cocq, ☎ 02 514 29 09.
Café Métropole, ✉ Hotel Métropole, place de Brouckère 31, ☎ 02 219 23 84.
La Chaloupe d'Or, ✉ Grand-Place 24, ☎ 02 511 41 61.
Dalí's Bar, ✉ petite rue des Bouchers 35, ☎ 02 511 54 67.
H20, ✉ rue du Marché au Charbon 27, ☎ 02 512 38 43.
Le Falstaff, ✉ rue Henri Maus 17–25, ☎ 02 511 87 89.
Le Food, ✉ rue Henri Mauss 25.
Le Fuse, ✉ rue Blaes 208, ☎ 02 511 97 89.
Kitty O'Shea's, ✉ blvd Charlemagne 42, ☎ 02 230 78 75.
Les Jeux d'Hiver, ✉ chemin du Croquet 1 (Bois de Cambre), ☎ 02 649 08 64.
Mappa Mundo, ✉ rue du Pont de la Carpe 2–6, ☎ 02 514 35 55.
O'Reilly's Pub, ✉ place de la Bourse 1, ☎ 02 552 04 80.
Roi des Belges, ✉ rue Jules van Praet 34, ☎ 02 503 43 00.
The Sparrow, ✉ rue Duquesnoy 18, ☎ 02 512 66 22.

ENTERTAINMENT
Nightlife

Brussels has a very dedicated and exciting nightlife, with something to appeal to all ages. Pubs and cafés constitute much of the city's nightlife and whether in Art-Deco or modernistic surrounds, the atmosphere is sure to be vibrant.

Tourists inevitably head for the **Grand-Place**. It has its nightly *son et lumière* per formance (*see* page 14), and the people-watching cafés around its perimeter are a great draw. Prices reflect its tourist appeal. Belgians will, however, head elsewhere. The area favoured currently by the younger set is that of **Place St Géry** (the other side of Boulevard Anspach) which extends through to **Ste Catherine**, while the **Rue du Marché au Charbon** between Grand-Place and St Géry offers both dining and drinking opportunities. Further afield, **Ixelles** and **Uccle** have a wealth of regular and favourite watering holes.

In between bar stops (including the city's numerous Irish pubs), Belgians will linger for the ubiquitous *frites* or waffles which have the useful attribute of providing a sponge for all that alcohol.

Opening hours for bars and cafés are in the morning, but the crowds don't start packing them until after 21:00. Most central bars and cafés close around 02:00 or 03:00. Discos and clubs are hardly open before 23:00 and will wrap up around 05:00–06:00. Best-known include techno favourite **Le Fuse**, **Le Food**, centrally located **The Sparrow**, and **Les Jeux d'Hiver**.

Around the Grand-Place, check out **La Chaloupe d'Or** in the tailors' guildhouse, a

good people-watching spot with views of the Town Hall, and then head, via **Dalí's Bar** (the surrealist hangout with live music), for either **H20** (a less raucous place for a drink and a bite), or the Art-Nouveau-inspired **Le Cirio** (*see* panel, page 52), altogether a more sober place to drink.

In the St Géry area head for **Mappa Mundo, À la Mort Subite**, which is also the name of a Belgian beer, **Zebra**, the fashionable **Roi des Belges**, or **O'Reilly's Pub**, which doubles as a home from home to the Irish.

Don't forget the Art-Nouveau favourites: **Le Falstaff**, **Le Cirio**, which numbered among its devotees René Magritte (to name but one), and **De Ultieme Hallucinatie**, up at the northern end of Rue Royale. For ultra-lush surrounds, stop in at the **Café Métropole** on the way and sup as one once did at the turn of the 19th century.

Further afield, **Kitty O'Shea's Irish Pub** in the European section of Brussels provides a good night out (and is the end point of Ryanair's coach service from Charleroi).

In the Ixelles and Uccle area, places to visit include the modern **L'Amour Fou** and **L'Ultime Atome**.

A Few More Pubs, Clubs and Bars

L'Ultime Atome, ✉ rue St Boniface 14, ☎ 02 511 13 67.

De Ultieme Hallucinatie, ✉ rue Royale 316, ☎ 02 217 06 14.

Zebra, ✉ place St Géry 35, ☎ 02 511 09 01.

Gay Contacts

Le Belgica (bar), ✉ rue du Marché au Charbon 32, ☎ 02 514 03 24, ⌚ 22:00–03:00 Thu–Sun.

Le Duquesnoy (bar), ✉ rue Duquesnoy 12, ☎ 02 502 38 83, ⌚ 21:00–03:00 Mon–Thu, 21:00–05:00 Fri–Sat, 18:00–03:00 Sun.

Tels Quels (bar), ✉ rue du Marché au Charbon 44, ☎ 02 512 45 87, ⌚ 17:00–02:00 Mon, Tue, Thu–Sun, 14:00–02:00 Wed.

English-speaking Gay Group, ✉ Boite postale 198, B-1060 Brussels, ☎ 02 537 47 04, ⌚ 08:30–22:00 Mon–Fri.

Tel'Egal, ✉ Boite postale 1969, B-1000 Brussels, ☎ 02 502 79 38, ⌚ 20:00–24:00 daily.

Left: *Pedestrian-only Rue des Bouchers provides myriad dining options.*

Cinemas

Kinépolis
Largest IMAX screen in Europe, 26 theatres, 4 suitable for wheelchair viewers.
⌧ Brupark, blvd du Centenaire 20
B-1020, Brussels
☎ 02 474 26 00
M Heysel

UGC De Brouckère
12 theatres
⌧ place de Brouckère 38, B-1000, Brussels
☎ 0900 10 440
M de Brouckère

Arenberg Galeries
⌧ Galerie de la Reine 26, B-1000, Brussels
☎ 02 512 80 63
☎ 0900 27 865
M Gare Centrale

Kladaradatsch! Palace
⌧ blvd Anspach 85, B-1000, Brussels
☎ 02 501 67 76

Musée du Cinéma
⌧ Palais des Beaux-Arts, rue Baron Horta 9, B-1000, Brussels
☎ 02 507 83 70
M Gare Centrale

UGC Toison d'Or
⌧ ave de la Toison d'Or 8, Galerie de la Toison, B-1060, Brussels
☎ 0900 10 440

Cinema

Great Belgian actors? Few, apart from Hollywood strongman Jean-Claude van Damme, have made it beyond their national borders. But that is not to say Belgium isn't interested in film; far from it.

Film-going is one of the great evening outings in Brussels and queues for new films may be long (reserve seats in advance). However, Belgian films are usually in French (some are in Dutch) and while they may win accolades at French festivals such as Cannes or Brussels, unfortunately they may not travel much further than their national borders.

Film-lovers should look out for Belgian-directed ***Le Huitième Jour*** (*The Eighth Day*), by Jaco van Dormael, starring France's Daniel Auteuil and Belgian Pascal Duquenne; ***Toto le Héro*** (*Toto the Hero*) by the same director; and ***Man Bites Dog*** or ***Taxanadria***, by Raoul Servais. Another Cannes winner was ***Rosetta*** directed by Luc and Jean-Pierre Dardene (the duo of directing brothers), a bleak exposé of marginal life in suburban Brussels.

Right: *The neo-classical façade of Joseph Poelaert's Théâtre Royale de la Monnaie.*

While home-grown films are sparse, imported ones are everywhere and the norm is to show these in English but with both French and Dutch subtitles (it becomes more complex when the original film was in none of these languages). Films change on Wednesdays. The largest two cinema complexes in Brussels are **Kinépolis** in Heysel with its 26 theatre screens, and the **UGC De Brouckère** in the Place De Brouckère, Lower Town (also known for its midnight screenings of new films).

However, there are other cinemas around town. In the Lower Town head for the **Arenberg Galeries** cinema in a delightful Art-Deco theatre with a very eclectic programme of international films; the **Kladaradatsch! Palace** (yes, that is spelled correctly), a fine Art-Deco venue featuring Hollywood and Dutch-language films; the **Musée du Cinema**, in the Palais des Beaux-Arts, which rescreens some of the greatest films, and in Upper Town there is the **UGC Toison d'Or** in Ixelles, which runs contemporary, crowd-pulling films in its 11 theatres.

Theatre

The country's most famous playwright, the Nobel-prizewinner, **Maurice Maeterlinck** (1862–1949), had tremendous success in the 1920–40s, and it is said that there have been few as internationally recognized since. However, for English-language speakers there is little theatre available, though the **Kaaitheater** sometimes hosts foreign fringe. If you can handle French or Dutch, ask the Tourism Office for venues and performance dates.

Theatres

Chapelle des Brigittines
✉ petit rue des Brigittines 1, B-1000, Brussels
☎ 02 506 43 00

Cirque Royale
✉ rue de l'Enseignement 81, B-1000, Brussels
☎ 02 218 20 15
M Madou

Kaaitheater
✉ Rue Notre Dame du Sommeil, B-1000, Brussels
☎ 02 201 59 59
💻 www.kaaitheater.be

Le Peruchet (Puppet Theatre)
✉ ave de la Forêt 50, B-1050, Brussels
☎ 02 673 87 30
🕒 Wed, Sat and Sun at 15:00. Closed Jul and Aug.

Théâtre National
✉ Centre Rogier, Place Rogier, B-1000, Brussels
☎ 02 203 53 03
M Rogier

Théâtre Royale de la Monnaie
Classical opera, ballet and concert performances.
✉ Place de la Monnaie, rue Leopold 4, B-1000, Brussels
☎ 02 229 12 00
M de Brouckère

Something Different
Fancy a change? The very popular **Kafka**, ✉ rue de la Vierge Noire 6, B-1000, Brussels, ☎ 02 513 54 89, serves up vodka by the glass, while **Le Cerceuil**, ✉ rue de Harengs 10–12, B-1000, Brussels, ☎ 02 512 30 77, is more the place for a bloody Mary. Its ghoulish interior (*cerceuil* means 'coffin') is appropriately decorated and pulls in the tourists with its chanting music, skeleton beer mugs and ultraviolet lighting.

Dance

Luckily dance knows no linguistic boundaries. Belgium has a good reputation for its dance, both classical and, more importantly, contemporary. Some foreign choreographers have made Brussels their home and created small dance companies with considerable success.

The three most important venues to stage dance are the **Théâtre Royale de la Monnaie**, the **Chapelle des Brigittines** and the **Cirque Royale**. The performances are very popular and so to secure seats for any of them, advance booking is necessary. The **Kaaitheater** is known for its arty work and sometimes hosts foreign performing troupes, as does the **Théâtre National**. (*See* panels on page 73 and left for all these contacts.) Lastly, the **Palais des Beaux-Arts** (*see* side panel) also hosts contemporary dance from time to time.

Music

Conservatoire Royal de Musique
✉ rue de la Régence 30, B-1000, Brussels
☎ 02 513 45 67
M Louise

Institut National de Radiodiffusion
✉ Place Flagey, Ixelles
☎ 02 641 10 10 (office), 02 641 10 20 (building)

Palais des Beaux-Arts
✉ rue Ravenstein 23, B-1000, Brussels
☎ 02 507 82 00 (box office), 02 507 84 44 (24-hour recorded info)
💻 www.pskpba.be
M Gare Centrale, Parc

Opera

There is no established opera company in Brussels – the Vlaamse Opera is based in Antwerp and the Opéra Royal de Wallonie is in Liège. However, opera is staged at the **Théâtre Royale de la Monnaie** (*see* panel, page 73) and tickets are like gold dust.

Music

The latest (large-scale) venue to reopen its doors is the boat-shaped **Institut National de Radiodiffusion** (*see* panel, page 74), once the biggest broadcasting studio in the world. It now hosts concerts of all types. This supplements performances by the **Ensemble Orchestral de Bruxelles**, the capital's symphony orchestra, and the **National Orchestra** created in 1936. The latter performs often in the **Palais des Beaux-Arts**. Chamber music and vocal concerts can also be enjoyed at the **Conservatoire Royal de Musique**. Jazz lovers also have a number of options (*see* panel on this page).

Festivals

Brussels' big day is actually a weekend – the second weekend of August. This is when the fabulous exhibition of potted begonias, the **Tapis des Fleurs**, is laid out in the Grand-Place to form a floral carpet.

The **Battle of Waterloo** is re-enacted every five years or so (check for exact dates with the Tourist Office). This large-scale re-enactment in period costume is spectacular.

More period costumes come out each year for the Medieval pageant, **Ommegang**, which runs along a route between the Grand-Place and Place du Grand Sablon

Jazz

Airport Sheraton Hotel
Noted for its Sunday morning jazz.
⊠ Brussels National Airport, B-1930, Zaventem
☎ 02 725 10 00

L'Archiduc
Weekend jazz in an enduring jazz bar.
⊠ rue Antoine Dansaert 6, B-1000, Brussels
☎ 02 512 06 52

Kladaradatsch! Palace
See page 72
🕒 jazz on Tuesdays

Sounds Jazz Club
⊠ rue de la Tulipe 28, B-1050, Brussels
☎ 02 512 92 50

Le Travers
Excellent jazz.
⊠ rue Traversière 11, St Josse ten Noode, B-1210, Brussels
☎ 02 218 40 86
🕒 open evenings except Sunday

Opposite: *Traditional dancing during one of the annual festivals.*
Left: *Musical instruments from another era appear at a popular festival.*

Did You Know?
The **saxophone** was invented by a Belgian, **Adolphe Sax**, who patented his invention in 1846. This musical instrument, either the alto or tenor variety, is used almost exclusively in jazz.

over the first Thursday to Saturday period in July. This procession includes not just costumed courtiers and nobles, but also peasants and horses.

The **Brosella Jazz and Folk Festival** is also a date to note. This July event is staged in the Parc d'Osseghem, Laeken.

Another musical theme is the **Nuits Botanique** held, mid-September, for a fortnight each year at the French cultural centre, in the botanical gardens. Music is played indoors and outdoors, performed by bands from Belgium and further afield.

Lastly, cinema buffs should head for Brussels during its **International Film Festival** (second half of January) when this two-week festival hosts both national and international films.

Up-to-date Events
The Tourist Office in Brussels keeps tabs of the best events on line. For this information, and other notes concerning prices, look up:
🖳 http://www.agenda.be
Cinema-goers might like to catch the annual **International Film Festival** in January. Check out the website:
🖳 http://www.filmfestivals.com

Opposite and left: *Period costumes are proudly worn for many of the festivals in Brussels.*

Spectator Sports

Football is one of the most popular spectator sports in Brussels (Belgium played in the FIFA World Cup in 2002), and **RSC Anderlecht** is one of the two major city clubs. First Division Anderlecht, ✉ avenue Théo Verbeeck 2, Anderlecht, ☎ 02 522 15 39, has a modern stadium, the facilities are excellent and any unruly behaviour is dealt with promptly and severely.

The second club, and one which has a better reputation but a lower rating, is the **RWD Molenbeek** (Racing White Daring Molenbeek) whose home ground is Stade Edmond Machtens, ✉ Rue Charles Malis, St Jans Molenbeek, ☎ 02 411 99 00.

If you're visiting Brussels during May, walk to the Parc du Cinquantenaire where the annual **Bruxelles 20km Run** (held on the last Sunday in May) has its starting point, before heading for the Bois de la Cambre and Avenue Louise, and then back to the park. It pulls in as many amateur competitors as the better-known marathon events in London or New York.

Anyone for Tennis?

Women's tennis may be dominated by the star players from the United States, but Belgium is also producing a new and promising breed of players.

For years **Sabine Appelmans** has played successful singles and doubles, while the current rising stars include **Justine Henin** and **Kim Clijsters**, both of whom now have top ranking positions in world tennis.

EXCURSIONS

Antwerp

Second largest town in Belgium, Dutch-speaking Antwerp is lucky that its old centre has survived and, in many instances, been restored (similar towns were damaged in World War II or neglected thereafter). The area west of the Grote Markt was once the portuary area, though this has now shifted northwards along the Scheldt.

The **Grote Markt** (**La Grande-Place**), a large cobblestone square, was formerly the commercial hub of daily life in the city, as its many 16th- and 17th-century guildhouses still attest. Most of these have been carefully restored and are now occupied not by artisans, but by cafés and restaurants.

Cornelius Floris constructed the **Stadhuis** (**Hôtel de Ville**) in 1564. Its façade borrows the best of various architectural styles and manages to combine them harmoniously, while its interior remains 19th century.

Along the banks of the Scheldt lies the Steenplein; **Het Steen** (the Stone) is a solid 11th-century castle surveying the riverine access to Antwerp. Here you can join a boat tour to see Antwerp's busy port. Today Het Steen shelters the **Nationaal Scheepvaartmuseum**, the National Maritime Museum, a haven for shipping and marine enthusiasts. Look out for the maquettes and memorabilia from Antwerp's Red Star Line that used to cross to the United States.

Walk back towards the cathedral via Vleeshhouwersstraat, which leads to the attractive 1501–04 **Vleeshuis**, the step-gabled guildhouse constructed by De

Antwerp
Location: Map H
Distance from Brussels: 50km (31 miles)
Duration: at least a day

Tourist Office
✉ Grote Markt 15
☎ 03 232 01 03
03 231 19 37
⏲ 09:00–18:00 Mon–Sat, 09:00–17:00 Sun
💻 www.visitantwerpen.be

Stadhuis
⏲ guided tours: 11:00, 14:00, 15:00 Mon–Tue; 14:00, 15:00 Fri–Sat

Scheepvaartmuseum and Vleeshuis
⏲ 10:00–17:00 Tue–Sun

Rubenshuis
✉ Wapper 9
⏲ 10:00–17:00 Tue–Sun, closed major public holidays

Kathedraal
⏲ 10:00–17:00 Mon–Fri, 10:00–15:00 Sat, 13:00–16:00 Sun and public holidays.

Waghemakere for Antwerp's butchers. It now houses a hotchpotch of museum items including decorative arts, weapons, archaeology and musical exhibits including César Franck's organ. **Oude Beurs**, nearby, was the exchange building and was constructed in 1515. It now houses municipal offices.

The disproportionately high tower of **Onze Lieve Vrouwe Kathedraal** – the largest cathedral in Belgium – dwarfs the building's surroundings and is visible from a great distance. Taking some 170 years to complete, the building was started in 1352 by Jan Appelmans, though as of the early 15th century his son, Pieter Appelmans, was responsible for its overall design. The remarkably light Gothic interior is a fabulous design of stained glass, chapels and perpendicular arches. There are a number of fine paintings, the most important of which are by **Peter Paul Rubens**. These include the *Raising of the Cross*; the *Descent from the Cross; The Resurrection,* with side panels showing St Catherine and St John the Baptist; and the beautiful *Assumption of the Virgin*. It is, however, the 123m (410ft) tower for which the cathedral is particularly noted. It was also the work of Appelmans, Herman and Dominicus de Waghemakere.

Rubenshuis, the grandiose townhouse (its decoration is very fine) in which this elegant painter lived, is now a museum and houses some of his works.

Lastly, Antwerp is noted for its diamond industry – and many visitors shop exclusively for these gems (*see* panel, page 9).

Who's Who in the Grote Markt

The north side of this square is the most impressive. Look out for the late 16th-century house at N° 3, **In den Engel**; the **Coopers' House** at N° 5 from the same date, and the tall **Archers' House** at N° 7. The **Mercers' House** at N° 17 is from the early 16th century. The Belgian sculptor **Jef Lambeaux** was born at N° 44 in 1852. And it was he who, in 1887, created the large fountain, the dashing **Brabofontein**, in memory of Silvius Brabo who is depicted throwing the hand of the giant, Antigonus, into the river.

Opposite: *The Town Hall in Grote Markt.*
Below: *Part of Rubens' house, now housing a museum.*

Boat Rides
This must be one of the most enjoyable ways of getting around Bruges in the warmer months of the year. Smallish boats starting from a number of different points navigate the narrow canals, taking visitors for daily, 50-minute, multilingual guided tours.

WWI Battlefield Tours
Quasimodo tours: laid-back day tours on Sun, Tue and Thu visit Passendale, Hill 60, dugouts, bunkers and Menin Gate (Ypres).
☎ 050 37 04 70
050 37 49 60

Opposite: *The beautifully maintained Stadhuis (Town Hall) in Bruges was begun in the 14th century.*
Below: *The Markt, a typically Flemish square now rimmed with restaurants and cafés, is the social heart of Bruges.*

Bruges

Undeniably one of Europe's great little towns, Bruges is an utter delight with its superb architecture and many picturesque canals, but it is one that is often overcrowded with visitors.

A tour of this historic town must start in its **Markt (Grand-Place)** – the social heart of Bruges. In years gone by it was home to the various guilds and the scene of the daily produce market. The statue of **Pieter de Coninck** and **Jan Breydel**, heroes of the 1302 Bruges Matins uprising, survey today's foreign visitors relaxing in restaurants and cafés housed in the historic buildings that rim the square.

Highlight of this large market square, and visible from afar over the city roofs, is the **Belfort (Beffroi)**. A climb up the belfry's 366 steps (a winding staircase that seems never-ending) will bring the visitor to its summit. At 83m (275ft) above the Markt, its views are superb. It was built in the 13th century to replace an earlier wooden tower and is noted for its 47-bell carillon, among the finest in the world. Concerts are played on these bells three times a week (Wed, Sat and Sun at 11:00). The adjacent **Hallen** (covered market hall) is likewise 13th century.

It's a short walk down Breidelstraat to the **Burg (Place du Bourg)**, an ancient political centre for Bruges. It owes its name to the defunct castle (*burg*) built there by Baudouin Bras de Fer (the first count of Flanders) in the 9th century. It is a magnificent square and one around which, among its elegant buildings, there are a

number of important sights. The **Stadhuis (Hôtel de Ville)**, at 12 Burg, is perhaps the most impressive construction. Very Gothic (1376–1420), it is almost fairy-tale perfect: a complex yet harmonious façade with niched statues, decorative architectural details and three slim turrets on its roof. On the first floor, the Gothic Hall is a magnificent meeting room beneath a polychrome and timber vaulted roof. Other buildings of note on the Burg include the **Oude Griffie** (the old Recorder's House) at 11A Burg, a 1537 Renaissance mansion which houses the **Brugse Vrije Museum**. Its highlight is the breathtaking wood and marble chimney piece, dating from 1529.

The **Groeningemuseum**, on the site of a former abbey, is *the* place for Flemish primitive painting, including works by **Jan van Eyck**, **Rogier van der Weyden**, **Hugo van der Goes** and **Dirk Bouts**, and has a fine collection of work by **Flemish expressionists** including Ostend-born **James Ensor**.

Legacy of artist Frank Brangwyn (1867–1956), the **Brangwyn Museum** is located in **Arentshuis**, a smart 18th-century mansion complete with formal garden.

The nearby **Memling Museum** is housed in the chapel belonging to the Old St John's Hospital (take time to look at the erstwhile hospital wards and the 17th-century dispensary). Although it has only six works by the Flemish primitive master, Hans Memling, they are superb.

Both the tranquil **Beginhof** and the **Cathedral of St Saviour** are a short walk from here.

Bruges
Location: Map F
Distance from Brussels: 94km (59 miles)
Duration: two days or more

Tourist Office
✉ Burg 11, B-8000
🕒 Apr–Sep: Mon–Fri 09:30–18:30, Sat–Sun 10:00–12:00, 14:00–18:30; Oct–Mar: Mon–Fri 09:30–17:00, Sat–Sun 09:30–13:00, 14:00–17:30
☎ 050 44 86 86
📠 050 44 86 00
💻 www.brugge.be

Stadhuis
🕒 09:30–17:00 daily, lunch break in winter.

Brugse Vrije Museum
🕒 10:00 to 17:00, with a 90-minute lunch break Tue–Sun, Feb–Dec.

Groeningemuseum, Brangwyn Museum (Arentshuis)
🕒 09:30–17:00 Wed–Mon

Memling Museum
🕒 09:30–17:00 Tue–Sun

Above: *Towering above the centre is St Baafskathedraal.* **Opposite:** *The guildhouses along the northern end of the Graslei.*

Ghent

Capital of East Flanders, Ghent is a large town and, located at the confluence of the rivers Lieve and Leie, the second largest port in Belgium. It was the birthplace of both Maurice Maeterlinck and Charles V. Much of its historic centre was razed for The World Fair in 1913, but some attractive patrician buildings still remain.

The pride of the city, **St Baafskathedraal (Cathédrale St Bavon)** was built over the former site of the Church of St Jean and manifests styles of the various eras in which the building took shape – Romanesque, high and late Gothic – to form a beautiful and imposing building. It is surmounted by a western tower which affords the energetic with panoramic views of Ghent.

Without doubt, the highlight of this cathedral, indeed one of the milestones of Flemish art, is the large polyptich of ***The Mystic Lamb*** in the chapel. It was painted around 1432, it is believed, by **Jan van Eyck** (and possibly his brother, Hubert) though art historians are yet to be convinced of this. Admire, too, the marvellous marble screens in the choir and the many paintings in the various chapels, among which is one by **Rubens**, *St Bavon entering the Abbey of St Amand*.

At the westerly end of Sint Baafsplein rise the **Belfort (Beffroi)** and Lakenhalle. The 91m (303ft) belfry, crowned by its 'flying' gilded copper dragon (an analogy for the power of the Ghent companies during

Ghent by Night
This town has a way with its illuminations which gives it another dimension. A walk through Ghent by night is an absolute MUST. All the major monuments are illuminated from sunset to midnight and, in the case of the three highest towers, until sunrise.

the Middle Ages), has dominated the city since its erection in the 13–14th centuries. Its carillon has 54 bells and these can be found in the Second Guard Room. Next to the belfry, the **Lakenhalle**, or Cloth Hall, was constructed in 1425.

On the eastern banks of the River Leie, the **Graslei** (**Quai aux Herbes**) was once the pulse of commercial Ghent. Some of the remaining guildhouses, dating from the 12th–17th centuries, underline Ghent's importance as a port. The best place to take in the whole of the Graslei is from the Korenlei, on the opposite bank of the river.

Continuing along Graslei, you'll come to the 15th-century **Groot Vleeshuis**, the meat market of yore. Cafés now occupy some of the stalls previously used for meat sales.

At the point where Ghent's two rivers meet stands the **Gravensteen** (**Château des Comtes**), Castle of the Counts – a fairy-tale complex towering over the water. With its round towers, narrow staircases, pepper-pot roofs, and solid stonework, it has served different functions since its construction in 1180. Used variously as a mint, court, jail and cotton mill, it contains a crypt, a dungeon and a museum which includes some unsavoury instruments for torture and coercion.

Lastly, try to save some time for the large and interesting **Museum voor Schone Kunsten** (**Musée des Beaux-Arts**) in Citadelpark. It has fine paintings from all eras of Belgian art including a good contemporary section.

Ghent
Location: Map G
Distance from Brussels: 55km (35 miles)
Duration: at least one day

Tourist Office
✉ Predikherenlei 2, B-9000, Ghent
☎ 09 225 36 41
Fax 09 225 62 88

St Baafskathedraal
✉ St Baafsplein
⌚ 08:30–17:00 daily (until 18:00 in summer); closed holidays and during services.

Belfort
✉ St Baafsplein
⌚ 10:00–12:30, 14:00–17:30 Spring–Autumn

Gravensteen
⌚ 09:00–17:00 daily (until 18:00 in summer)

Museum voor Schone Kunsten
✉ Nicolaas de Liemaeckereplein 3
⌚ 09:30–17:00 Tue–Sun.

Above: *Transport in Belgium is usually excellent. Buses are a good way of seeing Brussels at a leisurely pace.*

Fast Moves
Whether or not it is due to the European Union headquarters, transport in Brussels is excellent for a city of only one million inhabitants.

If you plan a stay of more than just a couple of days, get hold of the transport map issued by the Société des Transports Intercommunaux de Bruxelles (STIB). It is a comprehensive guide to all the métro, bus and tram services and you can work out your routes in advance.

Alternatively, surf your routes before driving or walking them. Visit 🖳 www.stib.be Enter your starting and finishing point and the computer will work out the fastest route.

Best Times to Visit

Early summer and early autumn are probably the best times to visit, as the weather is mild and often warm, making conditions ideal for exploring the city on foot. **Summer** is, however, considered the low season as the Eurocrats head home during July and August, returning for the new political season in early September. What this means for visitors is that the hotels, cafés and restaurants are less crowded (especially in the European sector of town which can appear deserted during summer). As the hotels have less commercial business, the rates tend to be lower and even discounted. As for the weather, it is at its driest (though never entirely dry) and can get relatively hot, though upper temperatures rarely exceed 30°C (86°F). It is far more pleasant to make excursions at this time of year. However, it is high season for European holidays and that means transport and sights are shared with other European holiday-makers (be warned that Bruges is full to bursting during the summer season). **Winter** has the distinct advantage of being out of the holiday season (museums and sights are far less crowded) but the weather is likely to be grey, sometimes damp, occasionally cold and the days are frustratingly short.

Tourist Information

For internet information look up the following helpful sites: 🖳 www.visitbelgium.com 🖳 www.visitflanders.com 🖳 www.tib.be
In the USA, tourist information is available from the Belgian Tourist Office, ✉ 780 Third Avenue, Suite 1501, New York, NY 10017, ☎ 212 758 8130, 📠 212 355 7675,

✉ info@visitbelgium.com ⌚ 09:00–17:00, Mon–Fri, and elsewhere from either its Walloon (French-speaking community) tourist office or its Flemish (Dutch-speaking) tourist office. In Great Britain, contact the tourist office at **Tourism Flanders-Brussels**, ✉ 31 Pepper Street, London E14 9RW, ☎ 0800 954 52 45 (brochures only), ☎ 0900 302 0245, 📠 (0) 20 7458 0045, ✉ info@flanders-tourism.org ⌚ 09:00–17:00, Mon–Fri. If you want to combine Brussels with the southeast of the country, contact the **Belgian Tourist Office Brussels-Ardennes**, ✉ 217 Marsh Wall, London E14 9FJ ☎ 0800 954 5245 (brochures only), ☎ 0906 3020 245, 📠 (0) 20 7531 0393, ✉ info@belgiumtheplaceto.be ⌚ 09:00–17:00 Mon–Fri. In Brussels, only basic information concerning hotels is available on a noticeboard in the airport (arrival concourse at the meeting point); it's much better to visit the excellent **TIB** (Tourist Information Bureau) in the Grand-Place, ✉ Hôtel de Ville de Bruxelles, Grand-Place, B-1000, Brussels, ☎ 02 513 89 40, 📠 02 513 83 20, ✉ info@brusselstourism.be ⌚ daily 09:00–18:00 Mar–Nov; Mon–Sat 09:00–18:00 Dec–Feb. For general information concerning travel elsewhere in Belgium, try the **Belgian Tourist Information Office**, ✉ rue du Marché aux Herbes 63, B-1000, Brussels, ☎ 02 504 03 90, 📠 02 504 02 70, ⌚ 09:00–18:00 Mon–Sat (closed 13:00–14:00 Sat lunch), 09:00–13:00 Sun Nov–Apr; 09:00–18:00 daily (closed 13:00–14:00 Sat and Sun lunch) May, Jun, Sep and Oct; 09:00–19:00 daily (closed 13:00–14:00 Sat and Sun lunch) Jul–Aug.

Entry Requirements

Visitors to Belgium from fellow European Union countries need a national identity card or a passport, valid for six months after the date of arrival. All other visitors require a full passport, likewise valid for six months. All non-EU citizens wishing to stay longer than 90 days will require a visa, though some nationalities require a visa for entry as well. Check with an embassy if in doubt. If you are driving your own car, don't forget your international driving licence (EU nationals may drive with domestic licences), the car's documents and the Green Card which provides insurance cover. This is available from your insurance company, and from the AA or RAC in the UK.

Customs

The maximum allowance for duty-free items brought into

Belgium is as follows: one litre of spirits or two of fortified wine; two litres of wine and 200 cigarettes.

Health Requirements

No vaccinations are required to enter Belgium and the only health hazards are the occasional upset stomach due to overindulgence. Belgium has a good health care organization and many medical staff speak English. EU citizens qualify for free medical treatment on presentation of the appropriate form (**E111** for British citizens). Visitors from elsewhere should arrange travel and medical insurance. Should a medical emergency arise, then contact one of the following hospitals with 24-hour emergency facilities: Hôpital Brugman, ✉ place van Gehuchten 4, B-1020, Brussels, ☎ 02 477 21 11; or Hôpital St Pierre, ✉ rue Haute 322, B-1000, Brussels, ☎ 02 535 31 11.

Getting There

Brussels is accessible by road, rail and air. **By air:** Zaventem Airport, 🖳 www.brusselsairport.be is just 14km (9 miles) northeast of Brussels. It is the home of the national airline and hosts arrivals of all major scheduled airlines. It is also the European base for Virgin Express. The **Airport Line** bus links the airport with nine major stops in central Brussels in less than 30 minutes, and departs half-hourly; ☎ 02 515 20 00, 🖳 www.stib.be Frequent trains likewise link with the Gare Centrale in the centre of town in 30 minutes, ☎ 02 753 24 40. There are, of course, taxis from airport to town. For flight information, ☎ 02 753 39 13. Inexpensive, no-frills airline, **Ryanair** 🖳 www.ryanair.com brings an increasing number of international travellers from other European destinations to Charleroi Airport (some 40km, 25 miles, south of Brussels) from where trains and buses shuttle passengers to Brussels and beyond. **By road:** The city is connected via fast motorways (*autoroutes*) to the coast, Germany, France or Luxembourg. Driving in Belgium is on the right. If you bring your own car into the country, a **Green Card** is necessary; third party insurance is compulsory. An **international driving licence** is also required for non-EU citizens. Hiring a car for a stay in Brussels, however, is not necessary as the public transport system is so efficient and the quality of driving is poor. In order to hire a car to travel outside the capital, drivers must be over 21 with a year's driving experience. **Speed**

Annual Holidays

1 January	New Year's Day	*Jour de l'an*	*Nieuwjaar'sdag*
March/April	Lent	*Carîme*	*Vastentijd*
March/April	Easter Sunday	*Pâques*	*Pasen*
March/April	Easter Monday	*Lundì de Pâques*	*Paasmaandag*
1 May	Labour Day	*Fête du Travail*	*Arbeidsdag*
May/June	Ascension	*Ascension*	*Hemelvaartsdag*
May/June	Pentecost	*Pentecôte*	*Pinksteren*
May/June	Pentecost Monday	*Lundì de Pentecôte*	*Pinkstermaandag*
21 July	National Day	*Fête national*	*Nationale feestdag*
15 August	Assumption	*Assomption*	*Maria Hemelvaart*
1 November	All Saints' Day	*Toussaint*	*Allerheiligen*
11 November	Armistice Day	*Armistice 1918*	*Wapenstilstand*
25 December	Christmas	*Noël*	*Kerstmis*

limits are 120kph (75mph) on *autoroutes* (which are toll-free), 90kph (55mph) on country roads, and 60 or 50kph (37 or 30mph) on urban roads. Wearing of seat belts is compulsory in the front and, if fitted, in the back. **Motorcyclists** must wear safety helmets by law.

By rail: Belgium has an excellent rail service and this is linked to the French and British services. There are several types of trains. The *Societé Nationale de Chemin de Fer Belge*, the **SNCB**, 💻 www.b-rail.be is the national rail company. **Trains** vary from the fast **Eurostar** (the inter-city London-Brussels service, or the Thalys Paris-Brussels connection, both departing from the Gare du Midi) to inter-urban. English is spoken at the Gare du Midi, ☎ 02 555 25 55. Check out deals too at 💻 www.eurostar.com Le Shuttle, ☎ (UK) 990 353535, 💻 www. 3eurotunnel.com is the service from the UK and leaves from Cheriton Park, near Folkestone, to Coquelles, near Calais. Good *autoroute* connections bring drivers to Brussels in around 1½ to 2 hours.

By boat: Hoverspeed ferries regularly cross from Dover to Ostend, ☎ (UK) 0870 240 8070, 💻 www.hoverspeed. co.uk Alternatively take one of the many sea crossings between Dover and Calais (💻 www.intofrance.co.uk for the best deals). Book in advance during summer.

What to Pack

Casual wear is fine for most occasions. The better restaurants require more formal dress. Remember sunglasses and a hat for summer, and comfortable shoes for walking around the cobblestone streets of the city. Show respect when entering churches.

Métro Art

While dashing in and out of the métro, take time to look at some of the modern art commissioned to decorate the métro stations (*see* page 48 for more details).

Inexpensive Sightseeing

Luckily, most sights in Brussels are central and the budget traveller can walk between them. However, look at the option of buying an unlimited daily travel card (very inexpensive) and, armed with a STIB métro/traim/bus map, plan out a route that crisscrosses the city and which takes in parks and museums, monuments and palaces. It does mean a little time is required but it's a great way to explore the city.

Money Matters

Belgium is a member of the EU and the **currency** is the euro. These are available in paper form in the following banknotes: 5, 10, 20, 50, 100, 200 and 500 euro denominations. There are coins in the following denominations: 1, 2, 5, 10, 20 and 50 cents, and 1 and 2 euros. There are **banks**, **ATMs** (distributing cash for credit card holders) and **exchange bureaux** all over the city. All major **credit cards** are accepted, although some places prefer cash. **Traveller's cheques** can be changed in banks and at the Bureaux de Change. Belgian **sales tax** (TVA) is currently 21% and is included in prices when you make a purchase. **Tipping** is optional; in most restaurants, diners round up the bill to the nearest euro. In smart restaurants 10% of the price of a meal is often included; if not, it will be expected.

Transport

Brussels' excellent transport system, the STIB (*Société des Transports Intercommunaux de Bruxelles*), is easy and inexpensive to use. The system comprises the **métro**, **prémétro**, **trams** and **buses**. The **métro** system (maps available from the Tourist Office and

Road Signs

English	French	Dutch
Road works	*Travaux*	*Werken*
Road	*Chemin/Rue*	*Weg*
Square	*Place*	*Plein*
Entrance	*Entrée*	*Ingang*
Exit	*Sortie*	*Uitgang*
No entry	*Entrée interdite*	*Verboden ingang*
Private parking	*Parking privé*	*privaatparkeer plaats*
Motorway	*Autoroute*	*Snelweg*
Keep right	*Tenez la droite*	*Rechts aanhouden*
Left/Right	*Gauche/droite*	*Links/rechts*
Closed	*Fermé(e)*	*Gesloten*

STIB stations at Gare du Midi) has few lines but covers much of the city. The best value is a block of 10 tickets for a journey (bus, tram or métro, and in any combination) lasting up to 60 minutes, which gives considerable savings over 10 singles. Or buy a daily ticket that offers unlimited travel on all the transport systems for 24 hours. Guard your belongings and if you are travelling alone in the evening or at the end of a line, think of taking a taxi instead. The **prémétro** is not the same as the métro – the carriages are different and it is more like a tram than a métro train. However, don't let that deter you – it works just as well. **Taxis** are convenient and not particularly expensive. They can be hailed on the street or found at taxi ranks at main intersections (De Brouckère, the railways stations, etc.). Some drivers speak English and all taxis are metered so communication is rarely a problem. There's an extra tax for travel with large pieces of luggage. Tips are appreciated but not expected.

Buses and **trams** run all over the city and are convenient ways to discover Brussels.

Train travel is the easiest way to get to other cities in Belgium. Frequent trains leave from the Gare du Nord, the Gare Centrale and the Gare du Midi. The same train might stop at all three, as they do in the case of the train travelling from the airport to the centre of town.

Business Hours

Shops and businesses generally open 09:00 or 10:00 to 18:00. Some **grocery-type** shops start much earlier, around 08:00, and work straight through to 19:00 or 20:00. Big **stores** stay open all day. Lunch tends to be served from about 12:30–15:00, with dinner from 19:00 (sometimes earlier for the benefit of the tourists) to 22:00. Bars and clubs stay open late (*see* pages 70–71).

Most **museums** are open 09:00–16:00, Tuesday to Saturday, invariably closing on Monday and sometimes open Sunday, half-day. **Banks** may open 09:00–15:30 but some do close for lunch. **Post offices** are open 09:00–17:00 Monday to Friday, and the GPO till 18:00. They are also open on Saturday morning.

Time Difference

Belgium is GMT+1.

Communications

The international dialling code for Belgium is 32. Each town has its own dialling prefix. When dialling from overseas the number for Brussels is ☎ 32 2 or when dialling from

within Belgium ☎ 02. The 0 is dropped for calling within the same city. The codes in this book have the 0 in front. When dialling a number within Belgium, dial the entire number including the area code even when you are within the same area code. If, for example you are phoning from area code 058 to a person who is also in area code 058, it is necessary to dial 058 followed by the rest of the number. To call overseas, ☎ 00, then the country code, city code and the subscriber's number. For International directory enquiries ☎ 1304; national directory enquiries ☎ 1307. Telephone cards can be bought from tobacconists or telephone shops. Prepaid telephone cards for local and international calls afford immense savings. **Mobile phones** operate on 1800 and 900 MHz frequencies, with comprehensive coverage on three main servers. The main **post office** (*La Poste*) is next to the Gare du Midi, ✉ avenue Fosny 48A, B-1060, Brussels; ◷ 07:00–23:00 daily. Info-poste: ☎ 02 226 21 11.

Electricity

The power system is 220 or 225 volts AC. Two-pin plugs are used. Americans need a transformer; British visitors, an adapter.

Weights and Measures

Belgium uses the metric system.

Health Precautions

Overindulgence in Belgium's rich food or its myriad beers is probably the most common health complaint. Drink plenty of bottled water and it will soon pass.

Health Services

The friendly pharmacists (easier for French speakers, though most chemists have an English-speaking staff member) will often advise on products. Chemists ◷ 09:00–17:00. If a problem persists, contact a doctor through your hotel.

Personal Safety

Petty crime is the only likely problem travellers will face. This is at its most rife on crowded trains, buses and in cinemas. Follow normal precautions: don't leave anything in a car and be careful with purses and wallets. Sexual harassment is not generally a problem and, as the city streets are usually so busy at night, women travellers should feel safe walking around town.

Emergencies

Ambulance and urgent medical service: ☎ 100. Federal police: ☎ 101. Anti-poisoning assistance: ☎ 070 245 245. Emergency helpline and European

assistance: ☎ 122.
Duty doctors:
☎ 02 479 18 18.
Duty dentists:
☎ 02 426 10 26.

Etiquette

The usual comments about decorum should be observed when visiting churches and religious monuments. But for the rest, Belgians are easy-going and very international in their attitudes.

Language

French is the most widely spoken language in Brussels; Dutch-speaking Belgians are in the minority here. Elsewhere in the country, more people speak Dutch than French. However, few nations match the polyglot capabilities of the Belgians. English is spoken (as a second or third language) by many people in the capital while many Eurocrats and diplomats who are posted to Brussels also use English as their language of expression. However, in the European section of Brussels, tableside conversations often run through three or four different languages as the different nationalities express themselves.

Useful Words and Phrases

English	French	Dutch
Good morning	*Bonjour*	*Goedemorgen*
Good afternoon	*Bonjour*	*Goedemiddag*
Good evening	*Bonsoir*	*Goedenavond*
How much?	*Combien?*	*Hoeveel?*
Thanks (very much)	*Merci (bien)*	*Dank u (wel)*
Good bye	*Au revoir*	*Tot ziens*
How much is...?	*Combien coûte...?*	*Hoe veel is het?*
Too expensive	*Trop cher*	*Te duur*
Where is ...?	*Où est ...?*	*Waar ist ... ?*
When does it open?	*À quelle heure s'ouvre t il?*	*Hoe laat opent het?*
Yes/No	*Oui/non*	*Ja/nee*
Closed	*Fermé*	*Gesloten*
Entrance	*Entrée*	*Ingang*
Exit	*Sortie*	*Uitgang*
I don't feel well	*Je ne me sens pas bien*	*Ik voel me niet goed*
Road	*Chemin/rue*	*Weg*
Square	*Place*	*Plein*
Café	*Café*	*Koffiehuis*
Chemist's	*La pharmacie*	*Apoteek*
Supermarket	*Le supermarché*	*Supermarkt*
ATM	*Distributeur de billets*	*Biljettenverdeler*
Town Hall	*Hôtel de Ville*	*Stadhuis*
Town plan	*Plan de Ville*	*Stadsplan*
House	*Maison*	*Huis*
Garden	*Jardin*	*Tuin*
Market	*Le Marché*	*Markt*
Church/chapel	*L'église/la chapelle*	*Kerk/Kapel*
Bike	*La bicyclette/vélo*	*Fiet*

Index of Sights

Page numbers given in **bold** type indicate photographs